CALLED TO
INFLUENCE

CALLED TO INFLUENCE

HOW TO BECOME A
KINGDOM-STYLE LEADER IN YOUR WORKPLACE

KAREN KIRCHER

malcolm down
PUBLISHING

21 20 19 18 17 16   7 6 5 4 3 2 1

First published in 2017 by Malcolm Down Publishing Ltd
www.malcolmdown.co.uk

British Library Cataloguing in Publication Data
A catalogue record for this book is available from the British Library.

ISBN: 978-1-910786-66-6

Cover design by Adam Jenkins

Printed and bound in Great Britain by
Marston Book Services Ltd, Oxfordshire

Thoughts From Others

Karen is a phenomenal woman who serves and leads in her family, church and business in an incredible way. Her passion for Jesus worked out so much in the marketplace is marvellous to watch. I've seen Karen develop first hand, growing in her spiritual and leadership gifts and putting them into practice both in her church family but also, perhaps more excitingly to me, in the marketplace. What we have learnt as a community Karen has skilfully reworked and packaged into a language that those in the marketplace can understand and begin to apply. I've loved hearing the stories, which she regularly brings back to encourage us all, of God at work in the workplace and how with courage and wisdom we can all change the world wherever we serve. Karen really has grasped what it means that we gather to scatter and that the church is called to be salt and light wherever she stands. I'm thrilled that you now get to share some of the stories and the thinking. These pages are rich with truth and encouragement and contain both foundational teaching on living our calling but also practical steps to help to activate and make it a reality. I hope you are as blessed and encouraged as I was to read these pages and hear from this remarkable woman.

Simon Holley, Lead Elder at King's Arms Church, Bedford and author of *Sustainable Power: Creating a Healthy Culture of the Supernatural in the Church Today.*

Called to Influence is a must read for any who are longing to see Christ's Kingdom influence the world around them. I have long respected Karen's ability to bring the presence of God into the everyday moments of life and to live as a prophetic outpost of heaven. It has been my privilege not only to watch Karen grow in her stature as a leader but to learn from her as a friend. She lives this book, through and through – it is an authentic story from an authentic woman. The stories and principles in this book will not only blow you away, but also give you a blueprint and mandate for missional living where Jesus has given you the privilege to lead. Read this book prayerfully, expectantly and hungrily – you were born to change the world!

Phil Wilthew, Leader at King's Arms Church, Bedford, and author of *Developing a Prophetic Culture: Building Healthy Churches that Hear Jesus Clearly.*

Karen has tackled the most crucial issue for me in terms of the perception of the Christian life at work. How do we see the place of the Christian in leadership in the workplace as opposed to 'ordained ministry'? Do we see the Christian at work as 'part-time' or as we would the pastor or priest, as in 'full-time ministry'? In the post-Christendom world the influence of the Christian in weekday activity is crucial and infinitely more effective than an hour or so in church on a Sunday. I commend this book to seekers in the place of leadership at work.

Professor Clive Morton OBE PhD CCIPD CEng, Professor at Middlesex University Business School, lay ecumenical canon at Peterborough Cathedral, Chair of Parish Nursing Missions UK and author of, among others, *Becoming World Class* and *By the Skin of Our Teeth.*

This is an inspiring and imagination-expanding book, with heart-warming and life-changing implications for Christian impact in daily life. Karen's deep grasp of our sonship/daughterhood in Christ, her appreciation of the implications of living in his kingdom, attentive trust, testimonies of his action and presence, all combine to open up new vistas for our daily discipleship and mission in God's world.

Mark Greene, Executive Director, The London Institute for Contemporary Christianity (LICC) and author of many books, including *Thank God it's Monday* and *Fruitfulness on the Frontline*.

It is refreshing to read a book written from a Kingdom perspective with God at the centre that communicates the view that Business is Mission. Karen has addressed some of the key issues of leadership, gifts and ministry which have been so misunderstood because of the negative legacy of the sacred–secular divide. It is easy to read, to the point and well-illustrated. There is an authenticity because it has been written by a practitioner of many years' experience as a leadership and organisational coach to the business world. Karen has bridged the world of people of faith and of none, bringing the heart and the word of God to both. The book offers many insights to help the reader answer the question, 'Where am I called to influence?' It certainly raises the profile of those in the world of work and my prayer is that it motivates us to encourage and pray for those in that sphere. This book is an absolute gem that for me stands out because of its basic foundational premise. I believe it will be liberating and empowering to all who read it with an open mind.

Terry Diggines, Consultant with A Call to Business. Previously Manager for Jaeger for men's and Area Manager Whirligig children's clothes (Coates Patons). Founder member and former chair of Newham Christian Fellowship and founder member of Transform Newham. Speaker at Spring Harvest and the mission group of Moorlands Bible College.

Acknowledgements

Welcome. I want to take the opportunity to thank those who have been a part of my journey over the years, enabling this book to evolve and become a reality.

Thank you to my parents for rooting faith and biblical truths into my formative years, and for their support and encouragement. Thank you to my wonderful husband, Mark, who has released me to go after my dreams, remaining steadfast in his love and support as I adventure with God. Thank you to my incredible children, Jack, Bradley and Georgina, who have taught me so much and also allowed me to go after the passions in my heart, at times at a cost to them. I hope this book will be part of my legacy to you.

Thank you to clients who have allowed me to journey with them as I learnt how to partner with God. It has been such a privilege to be a part of your development.Thank you to the many friends and church family who have believed and encouraged me onwards as I have challenged myself to explore how to be an ambassador for God and bring his Kingdom influence into my workplace. Phil, I appreciate how you have consistently cheered me on and provided opportunities to develop. Claire and Siân, your friendship and endless encouragement over the writing of this book are precious to me. Sophia and Jackie, thank you for the painstaking hours of editing on this manuscript. This book is better because of your input and I am so grateful.

Most importantly, thank you, God, for your unconditional love and pursuit of me as your daughter and for the fun journey we are on together.

Contents

Introduction: Influence as a Kingdom-Style Leader

You may easily discount yourself from reading this book because you are not in a formal leadership role either at church or elsewhere, so let's immediately deal with that in the hope that you will continue to read on. I believe,

> every person, in any given situation, has an opportunity to demonstrate leadership however small that moment may be.

It's about leading effectively and relationally in those situations. Children show leadership in the playground, parents are leaders in the home, teachers are leaders in the classroom, as are nurses on a ward and community officers on the streets. In whatever you do you will have many opportunities to show leadership.

> Leadership is key at every level and part of society and isn't just for those with a formal title or position of 'leader'.

More than ever we need good biblical leadership not just in our church environment but all areas of society such as education, healthcare, the media, government, business and the arts. As Christians, each and every one of us can be significant as a Kingdom-style leader during our lifetime, though some will go on to have more prominent, formal leadership roles.

To add context to these opening statements let me share my story with you.

As a young girl I loved to watch people. My father would say that, after visiting somewhere, I would be full of questions about what I had observed – why certain people looked unhappy, why others behaved the way they did. From an early age I had a hunger to understand the motivations of people but at the age of 21 was unclear which career to pursue. I headed to the careers office and found a possibility that felt like a good place to start: a role that combined shops and people. I applied for and was successful in being offered a place on a retail graduate programme as a personnel management trainee. That is where my career began: people watching and people management but now getting paid for the privilege.

In the early years of my career, though I believed in Jesus as my saviour, I did not have the relationship with him that I enjoy today. I certainly had no appreciation that I carried his presence and the power of his Kingdom in me in a way that could be a positive force for good in the workplace and life in general. However, I did carry an understanding of scripture and a moral code taught throughout my Christian upbringing about how to treat people with respect.

Entering retail management was a tough initiation into the world of business and within a year I found myself in a performance review for being 'too soft' regarding staff! Disagreeing with the feedback, I refused to turn away from the values I had been raised with around treating others as I would want to be treated and instead decided to express a different style of leadership, coming alongside and encouraging the best in people. I went on to complete my training, became professionally qualified and gained promotion to a senior role in Human Resources (HR) in a different organisation, before going freelance as a leadership and organisational development coach. Thirty years after entering the world of business I found myself facilitating a workshop for 35 HR professionals from a company employing nearly 5,000 staff, teaching them about collaborative working in a way that would honour each individual. In moments like that I stand amazed at the goodness of God and am so glad that, years ago, I chose to take a stance against dishonour. I love how God turns all things to good, taking our knocks in life to build our character and how he takes us on a journey to enable each and every one of us to have the opportunity to fulfil our calling and mission.

Several years after setting up as a freelance consultant, I was travelling home from an intensive leadership development week, feeling totally exhausted and just wanting to rest. As I sat quietly on the coach, God started to speak in a voice only I could hear. 'Come on, Karen, let's get focused; I want you to go out into the world to change the face of leadership.' People often ask how I knew this was God speaking and my answer is, quite simply, that with a vision that big it had to be him, particularly as my own thoughts were far from that place in that moment. Such a vision really is a question of 'I can't, but he can'. Whilst it felt scary, it was also exhilarating and ignited something deep inside my heart, which I concluded must be God. In those precious minutes he even gave me a new name for my business: Leading Leaders. It was exciting to get home and discover that the 'leadingleaders' domain name was available; that reinforced what I felt I had heard from God and set the trajectory for the next season of my life, which is still evolving. So, to the business world I am a leadership and organisational development coach but, in reality, I go into organisations teaching Jesus' leadership and the culture of God's Kingdom – I just don't call it that!

Over the past 16 years, as my relationship with God has developed and grown, I have gradually learnt how to navigate the often tough terrain of private, public and not-for-profit sectors, standing firm in hope and faith. Much of this journey has been learning how to bring alive the words in the Lord's Prayer: '*Your kingdom come, your will be done, on earth as it is in heaven*' (Matthew 6:10) making this verse accessible but inoffensive to those around. Most importantly, I have been learning how to love people through exercising covert and overt operations, rather like military manoeuvres on a battlefield, in order to reflect Jesus and his heavenly Kingdom. I have begun to understand how to stand firm as a Kingdom-style leader, which often feels so different to the world's perspective of leadership. My aim through this book is to share the journey in the hope that it will help you understand that, as a child of God and ambassador for heaven, you were born to influence. My thoughts, experiences and reflections from the last 30 years have evolved from an outwardly focused lens, living as a Christian in the world of business, healthcare and education, as well as a wife and mother. I don't profess to have all the answers as I am still learning as I go, but I hope the content will help you identify where you are called to influence and give you a fresh perspective and encouragement to go out into the world as a Kingdom-style leader.

God's Mission for You and Me

Hope in Jesus and faith in him encourages us to consider not only who God has created us to be but also how he is shaping us to powerfully fulfil the earth purpose he has designed for each and every one of us. The way that God has created the earth system and its processes reveals how he wastes nothing. Every animal, plant and part of nature is interwoven into a creative and orderly circle of life that is truly breathtaking. Likewise, God has created each individual to be unique in their identity and yet interwoven together we become an orderly and dynamic entity. We have each been given specific spiritual gifts: a heart that carries a clear passion for something or a specific group of people, with skills, abilities and experiences developed throughout life, all of which God predestines for use in the most incredible way. God wastes nothing, turning all things to good as part of his purposes for us.

Whether you are in a formal leadership role or part of a

team, permanent or temporary, full-time or part-time, paid or voluntary, know that,

> you have been sent to seek, love, serve and transform.

For so many years I sat in church wondering whether God wanted to use me because I did not feel called to full-time church ministry, to start new churches or to become a missionary abroad. Inviting friends and family to church on Sunday, special events and seeing friends become Christians did not feel like enough to me. There had to be more to the Christian life than this?

If I'm honest, because of that dissatisfaction I felt like a misfit, which is no doubt how Satan wanted me to feel because that way I remained disempowered. I am so grateful to have received the revelation that God's missional plan for each individual can sit equally in our everyday lives as within the walls of a church building. Please don't misunderstand me, I love serving my local church – we all need to play our part so that the church community can flourish. Equally, I totally respect those who are called to full-time church ministry. I just knew that was not for me and it was the church eldership that helped me to understand that my mission was elsewhere – in the world of business. Maybe yours is too? Maybe your ministry is in health, education or government and politics? Perhaps you understand this but need tools and tips to enable you to be more confident and effective where God has positioned you? As I bring this introduction to an end, indulge me by asking yourself two questions:

1. Do I acknowledge I am called to influence as I go about my daily life?
2. Do I seek to project Kingdom-style leadership to those around me?

If your answer is 'yes' to both, that's great and I hope this book enhances your knowledge and understanding of these questions. If, however, one of your answers is 'no' or 'not sure', I pray your perspective may shift as you read on and you will feel empowered and inspired to pursue your ministry as a Kingdom-style leader wherever God has positioned you in life.

I believe the real question we need to ask is: Where am I called to influence? Taking this a step further:

> How can I make the most of every opportunity to impact my area(s) of influence in a way that reflects the leadership of Jesus?

As God begins to reveal this to you, stand firm on the verse in Proverbs 3:5–6: *'Trust in the LORD with all your heart and lean not on your own understanding; in all your ways submit to him, and he will make your paths straight.'*

How to Use this Book

I recognise that this book may challenge your perception of what a Christian life can look like but I hope it also encourages you to reflect on your call to influence. To help with this, I have included a 'Discussion and Activation' section at the end of each chapter with questions to help you consolidate your thoughts and consider what steps you can take to put what you have read and learnt into action.

Although designed to be read on an individual basis you may find it fun to work through the chapters as a group, encouraging one another and holding each other accountable for actions you choose to take. Be prepared to be challenged, think differently and, most of all, get ready for all God has prepared as he calls you to influence as a Kingdom-style leader.

Discussion and Activation

Why have you chosen to read this book? What is it that compelled you to look at it?

What are your thoughts around the assertion that each and every one of us is called to influence as we go about our daily lives?

What leadership opportunities do you have as you go about your daily activities?

What are your expectations for this book – what do you want to learn and how do you want to be challenged?

1
The Backdrop: Society and Leadership Today

More than ever, good biblical leadership is required not only in our church environment but in every area of society. There is an incredible opportunity for each of us to bring about cultural transformation by positioning ourselves to influence as a Kingdom-style leader. As mentioned in the introduction, leadership isn't just for those with a formal title, position or authority. Whoever you are and whatever your role in society is, you have an opportunity to demonstrate leadership, however small that moment may be; it's about leading positively in those situations. We can all be significant as leaders, though some will go on to have more prominent, formal leadership roles.

So let's start to define and understand the world of leadership that we live in today. Leadership differs to management. Management is 'the skill or practice of controlling, directing or planning something'.[1] It is about planning, organising and coping with complexity, processes and procedures through the management of others. There will be management responsibilities that you execute on a daily basis, running a home, organising a classroom, managing the workload in an office or ensuring the smooth running of a hospital ward or department in a shop. Management is the world of doing! Leadership looks and feels very different to management; it is visionary: the projection of personality and character to inspire a group of people to achieve their desired outcome. This reflects some of the key principles Jesus exemplified in the way he led.

> Kingdom-style leadership is visionary;
> it is about character, relationships and inspiring others.

A successful leader is someone who understands themselves, the environment in which they operate, and the people they are privileged to lead. Seeing leadership as a privilege often causes a few comments when I facilitate groups of leaders. But imagine how different the world would be if all leaders saw leadership in this way across all areas of society, however tough they find their team, their situation and the future. Often the challenges of management take over but as followers of Jesus we need to learn how to balance everyday activities with being a good leader – developing healthy, happy and ultimately more productive people around us.

> Leadership is an opportunity to demonstrate an act of immense, humble generosity

...despite the many pressures modern-day living can throw at us. Over the past 40 years the world of work and pace of life has changed significantly. Job security is a thing of the past and has been replaced with a sense of career stability that comes from effectively managing your own work pathway. This has led to a more individualistic approach, with people travelling like hitchhikers between different roles and organisations, moving on when the time feels right or they are forced to leave due to redundancy or changes to structures and roles that do not meet their expectations. Thankfully, we don't have to travel this road alone and can lean on the advice and guidance not only from God but also trustworthy friends who can stand in prayer with us.

Alongside a more mobile workforce there is a much higher emphasis on profit, performance and efficiency with an expectation to deliver, because this is seen as the way for an organisation to survive against competition. This performance mindset applies beyond the world of business and commerce. For example, schools, the media, hospitals and the prison service are under scrutiny to meet the required standards set by Government. The world of work has become transactional at the expense of investing into relationships that are the heart of the organisation: those with employees, customers, suppliers, etc. In a climate of increasing competition, the emphasis becomes more and more about performance, efficiency and profit, and organisations can easily drift away from the original vision and design that inspired many a founder in the first place. Our nineteenth-century industrial heritage that was based on ethical profit can easily get lost. I love the stories of organisations such as Cadbury's, whose founder George Cadbury recognised that business is not a business unless it makes a profit, but that the purpose of profit was to give a man a job that changes his life for the better. He thought that 'if each man could have his own house, a large garden to cultivate and healthy surroundings – then, I thought, there will be for them a better opportunity of a happy family life'.[2] His legacy, and that of other godly businessmen who were part of the Quakers (for example Rowntree, Fry and Barclays from the nineteenth century), resulted in a regeneration and creation of various communities with homes, schools and healthcare that changed the local landscape for the better. Caring for each other through a sense of family that replicates the value of God's Kingdom is fast being replaced with a less ethical focus purely on money and profit akin to the realm of Satan. It is the very culture of targets, deliverables, compliance and regulation that provides Satan with an opportunity to add in his mix of fear and anxiety around not delivering what is expected. Directors and other senior leaders, who are under constant pressure to raise standards, also have to find efficiency savings and hit targets to satisfy key stakeholders. To achieve this, and compounded by time constraints and lack of leadership development, they can fall into the trap of focusing on managerial delivery rather than being the inspiring, encouraging, honouring leaders that people seek. Of course not all companies operate under the 'purely for profit' model and it is encouraging to learn about new studies that highlight the future of successful business being a combination of profit and purpose, with a new dialogue taking place on the role of business in society today.[3]

Tackling Busyness

The pace of life has been fuelled by advances in technology, which now make it possible to be contactable at all times, particularly when no boundaries have been agreed. The potential for long hours and 24/7 access makes it harder to switch off. Busyness becomes an accolade, not just in the context of work but in life in general. Think about it: when someone asks you how you are doing, is your answer, 'OK, but very busy'? When I began to notice these words tripping off my tongue I started to ask God, 'What is this all about?' He kindly shared with me that I had been buying into a negative belief that is rife in Western society today that there isn't enough time in the day to do everything I need to do. We go to bed feeling we have not achieved enough, sometimes tossing and turning as we worry about our to-do list, and wake up tired and fearing the onslaught of another day trying to achieve everything we feel pressured to deliver. If we are to shift our belief there isn't enough time in the day to do everything expected, we have to take a good look at the character of God the Creator. He is an abundant Father so why would God be stingy when it came to creating time and his balance of night and day? Ephesians 2:10 states: *'For we are God's handiwork, created in Christ Jesus to do good works, which God prepared in advance for us to do.'* Therefore it makes no sense to believe he has not provided sufficient time to do them. I had to repent believing the lie that God created time incorrectly. If we acknowledge God has given us work and sufficient time to complete it then maybe busyness is not about volume of work but what we focus on and how we prioritise time? You only have to read the Gospels to realise that Jesus was not only totally focused on his mission but that he never became stressed, anxiously running around like a headless chicken. His day was prioritised and sometimes reprioritised, to allow time to teach, socialise and spend time with his Father, and illustrates that...

> you can be productive without falling into the trap of busyness

...they are very different. Jesus was disciplined in his spiritual walk with the Father. In Matthew 14:13–23 we read how he combines solitude, retreat and prayer alongside his mission, on this occasion taking two mini-retreats in one day. The tragic news of the death of his cousin John urged him to withdraw by boat privately to a place of solitude. He then worked hard all day, healing the sick and feeding 5,000 people, which left him weary. So he retreated again, going up on a mountainside by himself to be with his Father.

Stress and tension run high as people try to deliver 'the impossible', which impacts on relationships within the work environment and at home. Instead of prioritising what is really important and focusing on these, we easily get distracted, filling our day with tasks and activities that add no value. Modern technology can be both a blessing and a curse if we are not on our guard in how we use it. The day-to-day hustle and bustle of life blocks our ability to stop, connect with God and know his Peace, but from this place we are best positioned to influence. We need to learn self-discipline around how and when we work, rest and play, whether we are called to influence in business, a classroom, in a hospital, church or running the home. God intentionally created day and night to cover 24 hours. If we remove 8 hours for sleep, how do we utilise the other 16 hours, being productive but balanced physically, emotionally, practically as well as spiritually? This will look different for each and every one of us but it is important to find your own equilibrium that you know will please God.

Unhealthy Leadership Styles

Over the years I have coached many wonderful people, from all levels of leadership, navigating the pathway of corporate success. What I have discovered is that it is easy to fall foul of one or a combination of unhealthy leadership styles, which negatively impact the leader, their team(s) and all their families. Whether you are in a formal leadership role or are under someone else's leadership, maybe some or all of the unhealthy leadership styles listed in the following table are familiar to you.

The underlying symptoms to all these unhealthy models of leadership root from the chatterbox voice we listen to in our heads, consisting of our negative self-talk and the lies broadcast by Satan. Such lies feed off our fear of failure, fear of rejection (demotion, redundancy, disciplinary), self-reliance (i.e. pride), control, judgements and un-forgivingness towards others. Like dominoes the effects of such negative thought patterns cascade down from senior director level, through middle management and onwards to the frontline workforce.

Performance -driven	Driven by targets, standards, systems and procedures at all costs. The focus is on results and undertaking activities, not people – both at work and with family.
Controlling	Keeps everything close to ensure everything is undertaken 'correctly' to stay on top of their game. No one is allowed to make any decisions without their input and approval. This behaviour continues at home or, due to the pressure of work, the home decisions are abdicated to someone else.
'I know best'	Refuses to delegate to ensure things are done their way. Believes no one can do it better than them because 'I know best', which becomes the pattern at home as well as at work. The corrosive effect of 'ego' destroys the potential for any self-directed team.
Overtime fanatic	Works all hours to ensure work is completed and targets met. Weekends and evenings exist to catch up so that the boss thinks they're a good performer. To maintain the flow of work, emails fly out around the clock, particularly Sunday evening, with the expectation that others will show equal dedication because that's the way to succeed. Home life fits around the schedule of work.
Always available	Phone and laptop on tap at all times, including when on holiday. Believes the world can't survive without their input but everyone else is active 24/7 so that's OK. Constant availability means everyone is reassured. There are no clear boundaries between home and work and relationships suffer.
Please everyone	Over-accommodates and tries to look after everyone despite pressure to hit deadlines. When everyone goes home they then tackle their work even if it means long hours and not being there for their family.

As 'followers' we can easily buy into unhelpful beliefs when working under one or all of these leadership styles, reflecting back to the leaders what they are projecting:

1. If I fail to meet targets I will lose my job and/or status.
2. Getting something wrong will reflect badly and weaken my position for promotion and job retention.
3. To ensure the task is done correctly I will have to do it myself.
4. Trust no one and watch your back.
5. Play the game and say what needs to be said, do what is expected – do not rock the boat.
6. If everyone is pleased with me then my position is safe.

As these thought patterns go up and down the organisation they are entrenched in the culture. It becomes the norm in the way things are done, without questioning whether they are right. Sadly, such leadership behaviour makes for unhappy followers, unhappy families and, if we are honest, unfulfilled and unhappy leaders.

> God's plan for work is that we are fruitful, not frustrated and fed up

...and that we get to reflect his Kingdom wherever we are sent. As followers of Jesus how can we powerfully display something different and more positive to those around us?

I firmly believe that most people set off for work with a desire to do a good job, collaboratively, alongside colleagues who hopefully have a similar perspective. Rarely do people set out with the intention to be difficult but often circumstances get in the way. We easily measure our satisfaction level from feeling valued and recognised for our outputs. Working *for* approval rather than *from* approval – because we believe a lie that God loves us for what we deliver rather than the truth that he loves us unconditionally because we are his beloved sons and daughters –

means that when our needs are not met we can feel unapprecia_ and become disgruntled. As Christians, we are favourably place_ through all parts of society to model something that is very different from the moaning and groaning, stress and strains that often occur around 'work' and the atmosphere that creates.

I recently heard a story by a gentleman who, six months previously, had heard a talk on the subject of influencing culture through changing the atmosphere. He shared with me how he had been deeply impacted by the notion that he had the authority to shift the atmosphere in the office, which up until then had been unpleasant due to gossip, slander and people just not caring for one another. He began to look for small ways to introduce a culture of honour, taking in cakes, making a drink for people and intentionally helping colleagues. Gradually others began to follow his lead and the atmosphere started to shift for the better. His boss noticed that something was different and thanked him for what he was doing. I love this story because it shows how one team member can lead through example and make a positive difference.

It's time to change our mindset that work is just about earning a living and recognise that there is a deeper calling and sense of satisfaction that flows from doing a good job that makes a difference to the world created by God himself.

Leadership is a reciprocal relationship between those who choose to lead, and those who decide to follow. Even those who have a formal leadership title face the reality that, if no one follows, they are simply taking a solitary walk on their own; it's a horrible thing to look over your shoulder only to discover nobody is there. Leaders who appreciate the reciprocal nature of leadership demonstrate the importance and benefits of teamwork and are inclusive, not exclusive, inviting others to participate in

This raises an interesting question: what do followers
...eader that makes them choose to follow? I believe
...attributes in any leader attract followers.

What Followers Look for in a Leader

- Provides vision and direction by being passionate and showing commitment to their vision.
- Shows enthusiasm and optimism.
- Demonstrates personal integrity.
- Practises what they preach.
- Develops other people, bringing out the best in them, focusing on the unique strengths of each.
- Recognises individual effort.
- Supports and actively listens to the ideas, challenges and worries of others. (They recognise God created them with two ears and one mouth and use them in this proportion!)
- Encourages teamwork.
- Actively encourages feedback.
- Is accepting of change (but not change for change sake).

Jesus demonstrated these attributes during his ministry and provides us with a practical and effective leadership model for all organisations, people and situations. There is no better example of leadership, and the good news is that we simply have to follow his lead. We can make the mistake of seeing Jesus as just a spiritual leader. This underplays his leadership skills, considering that he transformed twelve ordinary, and if we are honest, unlikely, men into the first generation of leaders of a movement that continues to affect the course of world history 2,000 years later.

> Our mindset needs to shift from survive to revive

...not just getting through the day to pay the bills, but taking every opportunity to bring about Kingdom and cultural transformation whilst at work. Wherever you are and for however long, know you are there for a purpose and reason and there is an opportunity to influence as a healthy leader and role model.

Discussion and Activation

Recognising that we can all be significant as leaders and your future may include more prominent, formal leadership roles, how can you develop your ability to see yourself as a leader?

Using the context of a team member positively shifting the culture at work, what small steps could you take to help make your environment a better place to be working in?

Did any of the unhealthy leadership styles resonate with you either as a leader or a follower?

As a leader, from the list of things that followers look for in a leader, which do you excel in and which do you need to develop?

To what extent have you been succumbing to busyness? What steps can you take to remove busyness and become more productive?

2
Called to Influence

God's agenda is not just to restore the Church but to transform culture and society through his people as they reflect heaven wherever they go, both at work and in their everyday lives. I believe this because this is what the Bible teaches us. God reveals how he loves to save, heal and set people free. In Matthew 4:23 we read how *'Jesus went throughout Galilee, teaching in their synagogues, proclaiming the good news of the kingdom, and healing every disease and illness among the people.'* The Bible goes on to make it clear that salvation, healings and setting people free are not to stop with Jesus. Our mission is to continue his work by going into the world to pray for people, healing the sick, bringing Freedom and releasing God's Kingdom wherever we go. Not to do so is to disobey God's plan for his Church as stated in Ephesians 3:10–11: *'His intent was that now, through the church, the manifold wisdom of God should be made known to the rulers and authorities in the heavenly realms, according to his eternal purpose that he accomplished in Christ Jesus our Lord.'* This passage of scripture is a rallying call for all Christians to seek to influence and transform society. We need to recognise that the Church is not a building, it is us: you and me. Therefore, we are the hope and need to reach out to everyone, not just from the confines of a church building or starting new churches but in our everyday living. The reality is that we live in a world that looks and feels rather broken despite the best efforts of international governments and politicians. So how can we, as the Church, more effectively bring the wisdom of God to rulers, authorities and society in general? In our daily lives, we have the most amazing opportunity to influence the world in a way that brings glory to God. With over 2.18 billion Christians worldwide, this accounts for nearly a third of the global population.[4] I can't help but wonder what the impact would be if every Christian not only understood but also walked in their full calling? What would be the impact if every Christian lived as Jesus did and lived the words in Isaiah 61, referenced by Jesus in Luke 4:18–19? *'The Spirit of the Lord is on me, because he has anointed me to proclaim good news to the poor. He has sent me to proclaim freedom for the prisoners and recovery of sight for the blind, to set the oppressed free, to proclaim the year of the Lord's favour.'* If this is the call on every life what are we waiting for? Is it fear, habit and/or misunderstanding holding you back?

The Sacred–Secular Divide

As Christians, our ancestry lies in the Jewish faith and our Jewish ancestors had a lifestyle that was holistic. Everything was under God's law and sacred. One of my favourite musicals, *Fiddler on the Roof*,[5] is set at the beginning of the twentieth century and follows the lives of a Jewish community in a little village called Anatevka. In one scene a young married couple are celebrating a 'new arrival' , and the village community gather together to welcome and pray a blessing. However, the new arrival is not a baby but a sewing machine for Motel the tailor. This scene illustrates the importance of giving any business to God and recognising the importance of his sovereignty over it, that by placing him at the centre it may flourish.

Whilst we no longer live under Old Testament law there is still something that we can learn from the way our Jewish ancestors and the early Christians lived. Somewhere along the way...

> we have divided our secular and sacred worlds

...making it harder for us to include and recognise God's presence in our 'work' environment. We have separated what we do at church on Sunday from our everyday lives, buying into a number of unhealthy beliefs that hold us back and slow down God's Kingdom from advancing here on earth as it is in heaven.

It is easy to believe that Kingdom advancement is for the elite few called to full-time ministry within the Church or those chosen to work as missionaries abroad. However, only a small percentage of people go into such full-time church ministry so where does that leave everyone else? Jesus clearly commissions *every* Christian to go and make disciples, heal the sick, set people free, and to release God's Kingdom wherever they go, so how do the rest of us go about achieving this? Having accepted the elitist principle, we have consequently bought into an extension of that: a belief that God has some sort of spiritual hierarchy. We have come to believe that he places sacred missionaries and church leaders right at the top and secular roles lower down in some sort of pecking order. Doctors and teachers respectably reside just below church roles whereas business, commerce and government are near the bottom. Where do volunteers or those who raise children on a full-time basis sit or do they fall off the scale all together? With such an arrangement we can easily overvalue or undervalue how God sees us and so have a skewed understanding of the worth he places on our mission of influence.

Alongside the development of this hazardous hierarchy, we have evolved a ministry culture that places most of its emphasis on only one day of the week through attending church on Sunday. Our Sunday service has become our 'sacred' part of the week when we encounter and praise God. What we do on Monday has become less important because it is considered to be 'secular'. However, the whole point of having a Sabbath day of rest is not to exalt that day or its activities, but rather the emphasis of the Sabbath is worship and thanksgiving for who God is, celebrating what he has done during the previous week and thanking God in anticipation of all his plans for the week to come. What a difference it would make if, full of praise and thanksgiving, the highlight of our week is the moment we leave our church building to go into the world for another week of mission. Many of us have been in full-time ministry for years, whether we realise it or not, but this has not been acknowledged by church leaders, nor by many believers because we have not seen mission in this way. It is so easy to allow the fourth commandment to be ignored or misrepresented but it was Jesus himself, spoken in Mark 2:27, who said that *'The Sabbath was made for man, not man for the Sabbath.'* It is the Sabbath's rest that ensures we have enough wisdom and strength to carry out God's plan, starting on Mondays when we go out to have an impact on culture and society. From this perspective it would be much easier to say 'thank God it's Monday' rather than just 'thank God it's Friday' because we are focused on God's mission. Such a mindset balances and values both work and rest.

In the UK in particular,

> we have bought into an unhealthy belief that only neutrality is acceptable in public.

Christians have become disempowered, feeling unable to speak out or challenge anything beyond the walls of the church building because we do not want to offend others. As we remain silent there becomes little difference in practice between the approach of believers and those who define themselves as 'honourable' non-believers. We save prayer and worship for our community of believers and family life, resulting in Christians ministering inwardly to each other rather than outwardly to others they encounter as part of their daily lives. Such an approach creates a bomb-shelter mindset: that it is better to take shelter from the scary world we don't want to offend rather than be the light on the hill, positively impacting on those around us. Recorded in Matthew 5:14–16, Jesus clearly teaches, *'You are the light of the world. A town built on a hill cannot be hidden. Neither do people light a lamp and put it under a bowl. Instead they put it on its stand, and it gives light to everyone in the house. In the same way, let your light shine before others, that they may see your good deeds and glorify your Father in heaven.'* I remember singing as a child 'This little light of mine I'm gonna let it shine . . . Let it shine, let it shine, let it shine.'[6] In our transition to adulthood, when did we think it was right to extinguish the light of Christ in us? The bomb-shelter approach to Christianity is a far cry from what was demonstrated by Jesus and how the early Christians went about their daily lives as recorded in the book of Acts.

What do We Mean by 'Work'?

To enable us as Christians to fulfil our calling, not only do we need to repent of and replace these unhelpful beliefs with ones that reflect Kingdom thinking, we also need to shift our perspective on how we define 'work'. We read in Genesis 2:15 that God created us and put us in the Garden of Eden to work it and take care of it. Our motivation is to obey his will, and while this includes providing for our needs and the needs of others, it is God's will that we are good stewards of the creation he has entrusted to us. We are made in God's image, which suggests that we must work as he does so that we can become more like him. We get to bear witness to his grace and mercy over us and to reflect his qualities as creator and redeemer in every part of our lives, both in church but also in our workplace. God delights in sharing his work ethic with us as we work together with him, bringing order and meaning to his universe.

Let's not get caught up with the fall of man that resulted after Adam and Eve ate the forbidden fruit, but instead seek to collaborate with God's original design and find ways to bring his Kingdom into the world. Let's shift our thinking and approach from just going out to work to recognising that work is God's master plan and a way we can have an impact on society.

How God Defines 'Work'

The more I have thought about this the more I have felt that maybe we categorise work in an unhelpful way that creates the divide between our sacred and secular worlds. I came across a really helpful biblical definition of work as 'the daily exertion, paid or unpaid, in contrast to rest and leisure, which is consistent with God's will, image and design'.[7] What I particularly like about this definition is that it values the effort put into all careers and callings equally and allows everyone to be honoured for their 'works'. It creates a more holistic approach to our daily lives. This is summarised clearly in Colossians 3:23: '*Whatever you do, work at it with all your heart, as working for the Lord, not for human masters.*'

God worked for six days and then had a day of rest. Similarly, we can look at our lives from the perspective that we are either working or resting. Maybe this is what David is referencing in Psalm 23:2: '*He makes me lie down in green pastures, he leads me beside quiet waters.*' This gives incredible insight that not only do we need to spend quality rest time with God but for the remainder of the day we need to let Jesus lead us as we walk together beside 'quiet waters'. It's from this peaceful, still, eye of the storm that we can feel the ongoing love and protection of God even though there are potential hurricanes all around as we go about our daily 'works'. It's from this place, as men and women of peace, that we are all called to influence.

Discussion and Activation

'The Spirit of the Lord is upon me, because he has anointed me to proclaim good news to the poor. He has sent me to proclaim freedom for the prisoners and recovery of sight for the blind, to set the oppressed free, to proclaim the year of the Lord's favour' (Luke 4:18–19).

When considering this Bible passage what is holding you back? Is it fear, habit or misunderstanding?

What unhealthy beliefs about church and full-time ministry have you been subscribing to?

How might God's definition of work help you move away from these unhelpful beliefs?

How good are you at lying down in green pastures with God (rest) and allowing him to lead you beside still waters as you work?

3
Where to Influence?

As we start to grasp the truth that we are all called to influence, the question becomes, 'Where, Lord?' So often we can sit in church waiting for a divine lightning bolt to hit us with God's vision for our life but, for the majority of people, it does not happen this way. This should not stop us responding to our call to influence, to go out and transform society. One strategy that churches have adopted is known as the 'Mountains (or spheres) of Influence', which details a way to reach various groups of people through various spheres.[8] They identified seven areas of influence, which can be easily remembered by the first seven letters of the alphabet:

A = Arts: painting, drama, sculpture, handicrafts, cinema, writing, dance, poetry, music.

B = Business and commerce.

C = Church (or Religion): includes social service.

D = Distribution of Media: newspaper, television, journalism, internet, radio, books, magazines.

E = Education: schools, colleges, universities and informal training.

F = Family: includes fostering and adoption, parenting and marriage counselling.

G = Government: includes law enforcement, Members of Parliament and the judicial system.

There are also other key areas that are outside these seven, including Sports, Science and Technology, and Healthcare. Whilst this is a helpful model we do not need to get too hung up on this; the point is that,

> wherever you are placed you can be a co-worker
> and ambassador for the Kingdom.

It is a biblical concept that we are called to influence. In the Old Testament, Daniel's life is testimony to how we can be faithful and obedient, bringing a godly perspective and excellence to those around in a way that brings peace and hope. Living in exile, Daniel was surrounded by a world that displayed military power and advances in architecture and technology beyond its years. Rather than bow down in fear to other gods, idols and the unscrupulous King Nebuchadnezzar, Daniel stood in faithfulness knowing God's sovereignty was all around him. As a result of standing firm and God protecting him and his friends, firstly in a burning furnace and secondly against a den of lions, Daniel was promoted to a higher level of authority in society. He maintained this and was able to influence across the land over many years. We can also make a choice not to become overwhelmed by the evidence of superior mighty and worldly values in society today and instead stand firm, expressing our faith and trust in God. Holding back simply confirms to people around us the view that Christianity is a personal lifestyle choice that's not for them when in actual fact there is an opportunity to serve, cover and redeem. We need to become dreamers, thinkers and activators who shape the world according to God's will and Kingdom. Within each church community, many are already involved with or working in a vast array of areas of influence. At my local church we actively bring together people with a common focus for their missions so that they can get to know each other, share collective experiences, learn from each other and, most importantly, pray and work together to outwardly bring the impact of God's Kingdom. Our desire is to act as catalysts to bring the love of Jesus and shift the atmosphere in each area of influence to reflect his Kingdom.

At an individual level you may immediately recognise which area(s) you are called to influence, but for others it may be more about realising a pattern over the years where God has given you different areas to influence dependent on the season of life that you are in. Whilst I know that business is an ongoing area that I am called to impact, I also recognise that as a mum I have an incredible opportunity to raise our children to impact on their friends and families as we live our lives together. If you are a full-time mum, do not buy in to the lie that your ministry is on pause because you are 'just a mum'! You have the same opportunity, not just for your children but those around your family as well, so that they may glimpse Jesus and his Kingdom from an early age. You will be one of the greatest influencers in your children's lives and have the opportunity to impact on many others and this is a huge part of your legacy. As a mum, I have had the opportunity to teach and nurture my three wonderful children but have also had many opportunities to influence the world of education, whether at toddler groups, as a parent helper in class, or joining a governing body as a parent governor at the children's schools. Don't underestimate the presence that you carry and impact you can have just by being a godly light at the school gates.

As a result of conversations that I had with one mum whilst waiting for our children, she appeared at our local church fun day and many years later is very much part of that community.

I love the story that Heidi Baker shares in her book *Birthing the Miraculous*.[9] In her youth she wanted to be a ballet dancer but an injury ended that particular dream. She explains that God had not blessed her with dancing shoes and how her disappointment opened the door to the opportunity for the establishment of Iris Global, a Christian humanitarian organisation that impacts thousands of children in Mozambique and other deprived areas of Africa. In her book Heidi asks: 'What shoes are you wearing? If you've been blessed with ballet shoes, then dance for God. But if he's blessed you with lumberjack boots, don't try and be a ballet dancer!'

Several years ago I heard a preacher share her heartfelt experiences of reaching out to various groups of people living in poverty, including working with prostitutes. Hearing this, I felt my heart break with compassion as God began to unpack the poverty spirit within the business world where many have prostituted themselves in the name of money, success, status and entitlement but feel unfulfilled, empty and alone. Up until this moment I had battled in my heart as to why others around me were so passionate about helping the poor, wondering what was wrong with me because I did not feel this to the same level. This message was profound and made me realise that the shoes I wear are designed to minister to the poor in business, highlighted in the Beatitudes in the Sermon on the Mount in Matthew 5:3–10.

Allow God to fill your heart with compassion for the people he calls you to reach, whether for a lifetime or a season of it. If, like me, God has given you a pair of business shoes then go and make a positive difference in business and commerce for him. If you have been given artist shoes go and enjoy being creative for him. If you have policeman's shoes or army boots you know what to do.

> Don't try and shoehorn yourself into someone else's
> shoes just because they look good on them

...they won't fit you and you'll end up with sore, aching feet, struggling to walk. Be who you have been created to be and make an impact where he leads you. Be intentional in allowing yourself time to really hear what God is saying and enjoy unpacking your designer shoe box with God. When you realise which tailor-made shoes God has gifted to you, put them on, start walking and amazing things will begin to happen.

Often people say to me how lucky I am to have heard so clearly what I am called to do, which enables me to focus. I believe God loves to share with each and every one of us and we just need to learn how to recognise his voice and pick up the clues along the way. The simple truth is that you need to prioritise time with God in order to hear his voice. Don't try to over complicate, miss or dismiss what you sense God is saying. Seek to understand what you have heard or feel in your heart. The good news is that when a vision looks and feels huge and totally impossible then this is a good indication that it is from God. We are not meant to be able to do it with our own strength. It should feel big. It will feel overwhelming and you will feel challenged around where to start. This keeps us in partnership with God. It's about partnering with him and through his strength being able to seek the treasure he has placed before us. This is clearly illustrated by the different responses of Zechariah and Mary (recorded in Luke 1:11–38), when they separately encounter the angel Gabriel. Zechariah's doubting response to the announcement that he will become a father and to name the child John was:

> *'How can I be sure of this? I am an old man and my wife is well on in years.' The angel said to him, 'I am Gabriel. I stand in the presence of God, and I have been sent to speak to you and to tell you this good news. And now you will be silent and not able to speak until the day this happens, because you did not believe my words, which will come true at their appointed time.'*
> (Luke 1:18–22)

Mary, though troubled by the announcement that she would be with child though still a virgin and the enormity of the child's future as the Son of the Most High, only asked questions to understand the calling on her life before responding: *'I am the Lord's servant . . . May your word to me be fulfilled'* (Luke 1:38).

My family has a tradition of not just exchanging Easter eggs but making this experience more exciting by creating a treasure hunt for each family member with clues along the way. This is so much fun as we each get to unravel the clues in order to find the treasure. I can honestly say that watching the kids work out the clues is as enjoyable as eating the chocolate (and anyone that knows me knows what a big statement that is!). Father God loves to place a treasure hunt before us and delights when we seek the clues in the hidden place with him illustrated in Proverbs 25:2: *'It is the glory of God to conceal a matter; to search out a matter is the glory of kings.'* As royal sons and daughters this is our opportunity and we must position ourselves in the right place to seek and submit to his calling over us.

Building the Plan

Remember, God wastes nothing, so all seasons and experiences build a tapestry of opportunity to influence. We just have to seek to see this through God's eyes, to see the treasure he is laying before us either as a lifetime calling or as a seasonal opportunity. Sometimes our call to influence can feel a little messy because we only have a rough perspective, a bit like looking at the back of a tapestry, which does not reveal the full glory of the picture at the front; but God knows the full picture and if we seek his guidance through prayer and listening for his voice, we will become more and more aware of the picture he is building as we remain obedient to him. One day, when we go to be with him, maybe the entire picture will become clearer; on that day he will ask us if we have done all that he asked and my desire is to be able to say, 'Yes, to the best of my ability, I tried to do this!'

Jeremiah 29:11 reassures us: *"For I know the plans I have for you," declares the LORD, "plans to prosper you and not to harm you, plans to give you hope and a future."* I have found it helpful to capture these plans onto 'truth cards', recording what God has promised and said either directly to me or prophetically through others, who I am and his plans for my life. I encourage you to be intentional around creating your own truth cards to help set the trajectory for your life. Any time you have a wobble or feel unclear, reread them. In your quiet time declare God's truth over them, praise God for who he is and seek his input into how you can take steps to move forwards. Put them up on a wall as a constant reminder of his goodness and faithfulness. Remember, 'I can't, but he can.' In your thanksgiving and praise don't become disheartened by what God has not yet done but continue to lavishly thank God for all that he is doing as the plans and purposes begin to flow. Let's seek every opportunity to tune into how God wants us to influence, to raise disciples and make him and his Kingdom known.

Discussion and Activation

Which area(s) do you have the opportunity to influence? Consider the seasons of your life that you have walked through and how this may shape the future as you are called to influence?

Have you been trying to put on someone else's shoes and, if so, how's this been working for you? How can you allow God to show you what's in your designer shoe box?

What has God already shared with you around 'plans I have for you . . . to give you hope and a future'? Record these on truth cards (and share with others so that they can pray and encourage you).

4
Who am I to Influence?

Getting out there, impacting on your area(s) of influence as a Kingdom-style leader, can feel incredibly daunting and the thought of this can activate feelings of fear and apprehension. You may also be thinking, 'How do I do this in reality?' Your starting point must be your understanding of who you are, because from the place of knowing our identity our mission can flow. I love the following quote from Marianne Williamson:

> Our deepest fear is not that we are inadequate. Our deepest fear is that we are powerful beyond measure. It is our light, not our darkness that most frightens us.
>
> We ask ourselves, 'Who am I to be brilliant, gorgeous, talented, and fabulous?' Actually, who are you *not* to be? You are a child of God.
>
> Your playing small does not serve the world. There is nothing enlightened about shrinking so that other people won't feel insecure around you.
>
> We are all meant to shine, as children do. We were born to manifest the glory of God that is within us. It is not just in some of us; it is in everyone and as we let our own light shine, we unconsciously give other people permission to do the same. As we are liberated from our own fear, our presence automatically liberates others.[10]

Our mission needs to flow from a place of identity where, first and foremost, we are beloved sons and daughters; otherwise our fear of under-performing or getting things wrong can take over and hold us back. Everything Jesus did would flow from his awareness of his identity as the Son. It was the first thing the Father made sure he understood before he embarked on any kind of ministry, illustrated in Matthew 3:16–17: *'As soon as Jesus was baptised, he went up out of the water. At that moment heaven was opened, and he saw the Spirit of God descending like a dove and alighting on him. And a voice from heaven said, "This is my Son, whom I love; with him I am well pleased."'* Reading this extract genuinely used to puzzle me. It appears in the Bible before Jesus starts his ministry and before he did anything miraculous, so why does Father God affirm his son in such a lavish way? My default response was, 'Surely Jesus needs to achieve something for his Father to be pleased?' Such a response highlights orphan thinking, rooted in the lie that you have to perform in order to get approval. My earth father was a wonderful man but he was not so good at openly showering me with love and affection. A 'well done' was my interpretation of love and this is how I felt his affirmation and approval. If I did well at school, passed a piano or dance exam or added another swimming badge to my collection I saw how pleased he was with me – I mistook approval for love. What I failed to see for so many years was that my earth father liked spending time with me, not because of what I had achieved but because I was his daughter. He enjoyed our time together, chatting and sharing common interests. I am so grateful that this penny dropped before he died and we had some quality time together. Let's not make the same mistake with our heavenly Father. The Christian faith is different from other faiths because not only is it based on relationship but at its heart is Father God's unconditional love for each and every one of us as his children. Even though he might not like some of the things we do, his perfect love neither increases nor decreases, regardless of our thoughts, deeds or actions. He consistently and lavishly loves us *because* he loves us, likes us and yearns to spend time together. We need to receive the revelation of our identity and relationship with Father God not just in our thinking but deep in our hearts.

The classic evangelical message of salvation, that if you say yes to Jesus and invite him into your life you will go to heaven for all eternity, has been thoroughly preached for many years. Whilst important, such a message only gives part of the picture in terms of what Jesus achieved for us at Calvary. Without a heartfelt revelation of our adoption (unequivocally God's) we easily fall into the trap of trying to validate our worth by creating a lifestyle of gratitude though performance. Even with an understanding of God's lavish grace, our desire to serve through performance can take over and lead to burnout. We come to him when we have done well, bearing gifts of ministry, when his desire all along is for us to sit and share life with him: our joys, our sorrows or just our funny observations throughout the day. We may try to hide from him when we feel we have not lived up to expectations, allowing guilt and shame to infiltrate and consume our thinking and actions. The result of a 'bad' day is to try harder the next or give up. Before we know it, we become trapped in a never-ending cycle of perceived underachievement and disappointment in our expectations of ourselves, the world around us and what we falsely believe about God. Such a situation must sadden Father God because this is not his heart. Our self-diagnosis of 'underperformance' comes with a list of symptoms that are not part of his Kingdom – namely, fear, lack of confidence and insecurity. When we grasp the completeness of not only our salvation but also our adoption, our confidence in God and who we are as his children, it makes us feel safe and secure.

> Failure in something does not make us a failure
> and is a wrong perspective to focus on

There are no fail grades in the Kingdom of Heaven, only Jesus' A-grade that he gave us as a result of his death on the cross; because we were given this 'A' we are free to live from this place, through our relationship with the most incredible, perfect Father. We become free to take a chance, to 'fail' in order to succeed in the future.

As a young child I loved nothing more than to jump the waves when we visited the seaside and the greatest thrill was tackling the biggest ones. On my own they were too scary and their force would knock me over; but holding my dad's hand or knowing he would lift me up if the wave was too big made me more adventurous. I was free to jump higher and bigger waves because I knew Dad would protect me and it was such fun. Our revelation as adopted sons or daughters of our heavenly Father is the same: he loves nothing more than to jump missional waves with his children, hanging out and having fun with us and protecting us as we travel through life together.

Birthing, Adoption and Commissioning

Just before Jesus ascended to heaven to be with the Father he talked to the disciples about the 'Great Commission', described in Matthew 28:16–20:

> *Then the eleven disciples went to Galilee, to the mountain where Jesus had told them to go. When they saw him, they worshipped him; but some doubted. Then Jesus came to them and said, 'All authority in heaven and on earth has been given to me. Therefore go and make disciples of all nations, baptising them in the name of the Father and of the Son and of the Holy Spirit, and teaching them to obey everything I have commanded you. And surely I am with you always, to the very end of the age.'*

We are also called to be part of the Great Commission and God calls us to help develop people as disciples and bring heaven on earth. To effectively achieve this we must,

> allow God to transform us from thinking like orphans to thinking like heirs.

As you recognise Jesus as your saviour don't stop there. Receive the relationship your heavenly Father offers you by getting close, intimate and real with him, culminating in the cry 'Abba' (Papa). In Genesis we read that on day six God created man in his own image and the first thing Adam saw when he opened his eyes was the Father's unconditional love, close up, as God breathed life into him. Adam spent day seven, his first day on earth, resting and enjoying fellowship with the Father before work started the following day. Once we are secure in our relationship as his son or daughter with access to him and his Kingdom, we are more capable of responding to our unique calling the Father has laid out before us. The more secure we feel, the greater the waves that we can jump together.

At my local church we keep at our core the 'Father Heart' message. Such teaching is essential to creating healed, restored, delivered disciples equipped to go out and have an impact on the world. It avoids broken people ministering to broken people! Bill Johnson, the leader of Bethel Church in California, describes this as needing to grasp 'Intimacy before Commission'. Intimacy with God is not the gateway to greater things because this attitude leads us back into performance. Living from the place of true intimacy and adoption is the greatest gift because it brings us into relationship with the Father and the revelation of his unconditional love and acceptance. It doesn't get better than this. The journey of healing and restoration through Jesus and becoming the adopted, beloved child of God enables us to recognise our value and significance, and provides the endless opportunities for us as his son or daughter. We rise up as co-heirs and ambassadors for his Kingdom rather than living from an earthly perspective. We must individually and corporately take this journey if we are going to successfully impact on all our areas of influence.

I was coaching a managing director when, 20 minutes into her first coaching session, I received a prophetic picture of my client standing at a crossroads and a question popped into my thoughts: 'Do you want to be a maintenance director or a pioneer?' This was quickly followed by a second question: 'What is your purpose, what has God called you to do?' I have to say total fear gripped me but, after an internal debate with God, I realised the worst thing to happen would be a rapid exit from the premises, and I knew in that moment I had to make the decision to face my client's potential disapproval rather than be disobedient to God. So I took a deep breath and said, 'This might sound totally crazy, but I am a Christian who believes God speaks today and I feel that he wants me to ask you this question: What is your purpose here on earth?' There was an awkward pause followed by her response: 'Wow, I was not expecting that!' Our conversation shifted to a whole new level as she shared with me that she was a Christian and we started visioning the concept of being a pioneer and the relevance of the crossroads picture that I had received for her.

Had I not felt totally secure in my identity as a beloved daughter and focused on the Father's provision and protection, I would never have been obedient to the Holy Spirit and my client would not have received such a revelation from her Father in heaven.

Knowing your identity as a son or daughter and understanding God's truth from reading the Bible builds self-worth. It enables you to be free to say to yourself: I am therefore I do, not the other way around!' Jesus always knows he is his Father's son.

He never worries about what people think or whether they like him or not and this prevents him from caving in to fear. Romans 8:14–15 teaches us that *'those who are led by the Spirit of God are the children of God. The spirit you received does not make you slaves, so that you live in fear again; rather, the Spirit you received brought about your adoption to sonship. And by him we cry, "Abba Father."'* Chaos can so easily ensue where the glue of God's truth gets removed because it holds life together and enables us to drive forward from a place of wholeness. I love that the Bible shouts so loudly, 'God loves me!' When I read his Word my desire is to hear his voice and feel his heartbeat because I need such intimacy and healing before any Kingdom works can bear fruit. His Word really is the food that enables life. God is a Father who is intimate, inclusive to all and infinite. I get to call him Dad from a place of respect and reverence, recognising him as all-powerful, all-knowing, mighty God, 'Hallowed be your name'. Angels get to call him Holy but I get to call him Abba Father (Papa).

> When I sit with him any trace of evil in my thinking gets hugged out of me

...by the most amazing Dad as his truth and love pour in. From this place I get to be part of his army, working from approval, not for approval. We get the opportunity to deepen our 'son-ship' or 'daughterhood' and enjoy the relationship as co-heirs with Jesus. No wonder Satan will do all he can to prevent this. Think about it: if you were Satan, you would do anything you could to blow a Christian off course from realising their true identity. You would use lies, obstacles and distractions, anything to stop a beloved child of God discovering who they really are. As Satan you would go all out to do this because you know that even the strongest gates of his kingdom, i.e. hell, can't withstand the unified, glorified, mobilised sons or daughters of God, collectively known as 'the bride of Jesus Christ'; once the gates are breached many of Satan's prisoners will be set free. Through knowing and accepting our identity we are incredibly dangerous for the Kingdom in the eyes of Satan. If Satan is silent in your life, either you have totally mastered the ability to focus completely on God or Satan is not bothering to transmit anything to you because he currently does not see you as a threat. When he does try to deceive or cause havoc remember Jesus' response to the disciples in Matthew 26:53: *'Do you think I cannot call on my Father, and he will at once put at my disposal more than twelve legions of angels?'* When we call out to God, he can do the same for us because we are his beloved children.

It's time to grasp the truth. Father God chose you, adopted you and has given you total access to all that he has through your adoption. You are able to walk in his unconditional favour, acceptance and love. You have a new family including the most incredible big brother who chose not only to die for you on the cross so that you could know his Father intimately, but also share his entire inheritance as he looks out for you and intercedes on your behalf. God sings over you and not only loves you but also likes you enormously. His ideal day is to hang out with you, so you can enjoy each other's company as you adventure and jump the waves together. You get to do this knowing Father God will protect and endlessly provide along the way, not just your basic needs but lavishly. From this place you can walk with a feeling of security, love and peace that indeed passes all understanding.

For I am convinced that neither death nor life, neither angels nor demons, neither the present nor the future, nor any powers, neither height nor depth, nor anything else in all creation, will be able to separate us from the love of God that is in Christ Jesus our Lord. (Romans 8:38–39)

Declarations: Who I Am in Him

Use the following truths as weapons to declare over yourself, particularly if you are battling your identity or facing difficult workplace or life situations. There is something powerful about affirming them aloud in your quiet time with God or when you are travelling to or from work.

Be aware of God's truths that you struggle with as this may give you a good place to start as part of your inner healing and acceptance of your identity. God wants you to receive deep in your heart all the truths below, not just a pick-and-mix selection of them:

Essential Truths.

I am fearfully and wonderfully made; your works are wonderful, I know that full well. (Psalm 139:14)

I am a new creation in Christ – the old me has died and I am now a brand new person! (2 Corinthians 5:17)

I am Holy in God's sight. Without blemish and free from accusation. (Colossians 1:22)

I am no longer under any condemnation. God is never ashamed of me! (Romans 8:1)

I am in Christ and he is in me! (John 14:20)

I am a son/daughter of the King. I am royalty! (1 John 3:1)

I am a saint. (Ephesians 1:1 and other multiple references)

I have been raised up with Christ and I'm now seated with him in heavenly places. (Ephesians 2:6)

I am an heir of God and a co-heir with Christ. (Romans 8:17)

I am an ambassador of Christ. (2 Corinthians 5:20)

I am being transformed into the image of Christ from one degree of glory to another. (2 Corinthians 3:18)

I cannot be separated from the Father's love. (Romans 8:35)

On the cross Jesus cried, 'It is finished!' In this declaration he seized his God-given destiny and succeeded in carrying out the unique work his Father gave him. This revelation enables us to influence without striving. We walk in the love of God and, through the overflow of his love, can give it away. It is not about what we do but what Jesus achieved on the cross. We are not just forgiven, but free to be, as beloved children of God.

A few years ago God gave me a word that, as a child of God, we get to carry the DNA of Jesus Christ and this is what I recorded in my journal: 'I am taking you beyond your righteous robe and ring that you received through adoption as my (son or) daughter and I am bringing you into a fresh revelation beyond your adoption into my family. For my heart's desire is for you to walk in the truth not only of who you are in me, justified through the cross, but that this truth reconciles you to receiving the Holy Spirit. Who you are goes beyond adoption because children who are adopted can feel they are not really a part of their adopted family because they are not biologically related. This is my revelation to you: you are my child, not just by adoption but because the Holy Spirit is my Spirit and you can ask my Spirit to live deep within you. The Holy Spirit is my very being, my DNA. Receive my Holy Spirit, my DNA, receive all of me.'

If we are to go out and influence society we need to live from the right side of the cross, living from the perspective of his resurrection victory. Christ's ascension to heaven made it possible for the Holy Spirit to come and dwell here on earth, Christ's very DNA to be deep within us. Cars only run when they have fuel and we need to keep close to God and continuously fill up spiritually every day by inviting the Holy Spirit in. Our ministry flows out of acceptance and love through intimacy with the Father. We have full access to him and his throne just by being his son or daughter because of the power of the cross and his Spirit dwelling in us. What an incredible opportunity we have to enjoy such a beautiful relationship and from this place our ministry can flow outwards. Let's not just settle for the message of salvation, clasping our golden ticket to heaven for when God calls us home. What a wasted opportunity that will be. Let's grasp the enormity of Christ's sacrifice on the cross that enables us to enjoy such deep intimacy with Father God, freely walking with him as beloved, adopted sons and daughters with access to the Kingdom and his authority to transform society around us as we go about our daily lives.

Discussion and Activation

What is the foundation for your calling? Do you know Abba's acceptance and love or do you strive to earn them?

What stage of your Christian journey have you reached in terms of recognising (birthing), receiving (adoption) and responding (commissioning)? What might help you to progress further?

From the list of declarations, which do you find easiest and hardest to declare? Consider why that might be and who you can walk with to help you overcome any associated lies, hurts, habits or hang-ups that get in your way? (The 'Relational Leader' chapters will also help.)

Are you living from the right side of the cross i.e. Christ's resurrection victory? Read Revelation 1:9–18 to visualise Christ in his full glory. What steps can you take to live from this victory place?

How good are you at refuelling with the Holy Spirit? Do you run on half-full, half-empty or risk running out altogether? What steps can you take to be regularly topped-up by spending more time with the Holy Spirit?

5

How to Influence: From a Kingdom Perspective

When Jesus came to earth just over 2,000 years ago he taught his followers to pray: *'Our Father in heaven, hallowed be your name, your kingdom come, your will be done, on earth as it is in heaven'* (Matthew 6:9–10). *'On earth as it is in heaven'* became a co-existing reality when Jesus came to earth. As sons and daughters we now have access to God's Kingdom, though we recognise we will not experience its fullness until Jesus returns. This passage from the Lord's Prayer, recorded in the Gospels of Matthew and Luke, is a call for the roots of God's Kingdom to be restored through a different approach by the Church in preparation for Jesus' return. It is not enough to relax in our salvation, sure that we have our ticket through the pearly gates into heaven when we die. Nor can we live with the aforementioned bomb-shelter church building mindset, hiding safely from the horrors around us until we are called home to heaven. We must guard against developing an inward charismatic bubble, enjoying the experience of God's Kingdom presence just for ourselves rather than taking it outwards as he intended. We need to learn how to influence from a Kingdom perspective.

To go out and bring cultural transformation in our area(s) of influence requires us to understand what 'kingdom come' really means? In the early days of Christianity, when Jesus started to talk about the Kingdom being at hand, his Jewish audience knew exactly what he was talking about because of their knowledge of the words spoken by the prophet Isaiah recorded in the Old

Testament. After some astonishing announcements by John the Baptist to *'Repent for the kingdom of heaven has come near'* (Matthew 3:2), there before them was a man named Jesus declaring that the Kingdom of God was not only at hand but that their long-awaited Messiah was standing there before them (Luke 4:16–21). I can only imagine what it must have been like for the people gathered around him in that moment. For over 400 hundred years God had been silent (the gap between the end of the Old Testament and the beginning of the New Testament). Through these years the Jewish people had waited for the Messiah and his Kingdom to come and rescue them and they must have been in a complete state of shock, astonishment and excitement that was palpable. Over the years our understanding of the Kingdom has eroded, like cliffs disappearing into the sea, changing the landscape of our faith.

Teaching has focused on God (the King) but not the fullness of his Kingdom. You can't have one without the other, and the good news is that we can experience both. I have heard many a good sermon explain that you can't truly love Christ if you don't also love his Church because Christ is the head and the Church is his body. We also need quality teaching that knowing the King means we get to enjoy his Kingdom. As his beloved sons and daughters we have the highest security clearance into the heavenly realm; indeed, his Kingdom is at hand. Quite often in sermons Kingdom is limited to just Salvation and Healing, both of which are important but only give part of the picture. When Jesus talks about KINGDOM he is referencing Isaiah 61 that outlines the signs of the Kingdom: SALVATION and HEALING but he is equally talking about FREEDOM (Deliverance), PEACE, JOY, JUSTICE (Righteousness), GOD'S PRESENCE and his COMFORT. In our daily lives we have the opportunity to powerfully tap into all of these and call them down from heaven as we encounter people in our area(s) of influence.

I had one client arrive at a coaching session very burdened by things going on in her life, exclaiming that she just wanted to find peace. I explained that God's Peace is available at any time if she would like me to 'pray it down', to which she replied 'yes please'. Both of us felt the tangible presence of Peace fill the room, which she had never experienced before. A week later her boss asked what had happened in her coaching as she was so different, 'like she is walking on a peaceful happy cloud!'

As we grasp what Kingdom is all about we can seek to understand God's design for our area(s) of influence. I often ponder the question 'What will the world of business look like in heaven?' because I want to pray for this and call it down from heaven to earth to shift the atmosphere to reflect God's Kingdom.

I regularly run leadership development programmes in a variety of organisations. On the first day of one particular programme with a senior management team I began challenging them on the standards of behaviour they wanted to adopt for the time we had together in the hope that this would evolve into a cultural standard in the workplace. This was a discussion I regularly include and the responses were consistently around respect: not talking over each other, valuing different opinions, etc. At my local church we have, as one of our values, a Kingdom principle around the culture of honour, so within the first hour of this particular programme I shared this concept with the group. I explained that 'to honour' means to respect and hold in high esteem.[11] When we honour someone, it gives an opportunity through our words and actions to declare that we see the individual to be worthy and amounting to something. I challenged them to create a culture of honour in which they could honestly say that 'we choose at all times and at all levels to recognise, acknowledge worth and to act accordingly with each other through mutual respect, honesty and sincerity'. They loved it! At the end of their six-month leadership programme it was the culture of honour that they chose to take forward as one of their key learning points.

I see this repeated time and time again with workplace clients; they hanker after a different way of being with each other. I privately pray and call it from heaven. I declare it into the meeting rooms and into their offices. It can make such a difference to the way a senior team operates if they embrace this concept and make it a part of their culture. It becomes a piece of heaven on earth.

When working in healthcare it is easy to picture God's design because in heaven there is no sickness, pain or suffering. This is what I pray for and call down in order to shift the atmosphere to reflect God's Kingdom.

Whilst working on a contract within an NHS Trust I regularly took the opportunity to play worship music in the office and walked the corridors, quietly praying and declaring 'your Kingdom come'. I am always very intentional around this type of prayer, even if I am just visiting someone in hospital, because I recognise the amazing Creator of all medicine and healing and that his Kingdom is available to all those who ask. There is no limit to God's goodness and ability to heal either supernaturally in that moment or through skilled doctors and nurses.

Once we understand and focus on Kingdom values and recognising through our identity that we have access to them, the opposite of these Kingdom values become a target for our attention on earth as we learn to pray and take authority over them. If you come up against anger, you can pray for Peace, when you find despair you pray for Comfort, when there is hopelessness and heaviness then seek Hope and Joy. Praying for God's presence can change any situation.

I feel challenged by the often-used sentiment: 'Preach at all times and only use words when you have to.' Such a statement makes me consider how I am and how I behave every day – does this 'preach' the gospel? In my workplace, if I am the first living representation of the Bible that people 'read', what impression will they get about Jesus? Do I reflect 'on earth as it is in heaven'? The way I go about my day-to-day business,

> do people around me catch a glimpse of the Father's love?

We need to recognise that we express the thoughts that fill our consciousness, which means we need to fill our every thought with the truth of the Kingdom. What we believe impacts what we think, which then impacts how we behave and respond to situations and people around us.

Over a number of years I had the privilege of coaching one particular senior manager and did so from a Kingdom perspective, loving him in a way that I felt Jesus would want me to care for him every time we met. Not long after his father sadly died, he shared with me that he'd recently had three dreams that he did not understand and didn't know whether they were connected or why they were in such Technicolor. I explained that I was happy to interpret but could only do so from a Christian context. The first dream was of him being held by his dad as a baby. In the second he was a young adult in a bar with his dad chatting away and enjoying each other's company. The third was very different; he was walking down a darkened street and heard a screeching of brakes and a voice, his father's, shout out, 'It's OK, I've got your back.'

As he confided in me I could feel the presence of the Holy Spirit and gave the interpretation that all three were about the love of both his fathers and that Father God is there for him in the same way that his dad had always been. This was an emotional, revelatory moment and the peace and comfort of the Kingdom broke in. Six weeks later he told me that his niece, who lived hundreds of miles away, had sent for his birthday a framed picture of him as a baby and the photo was identical to his first dream. This opened the door to very frank conversations about faith as he became increasingly aware of his feelings of peace, contentment and 'being' that felt very different to his previous pattern of proving himself and constantly 'doing'. Subsequently, he made steps on his journey of faith, realising that Christianity is not about religion but relationships. His journey continues and I hope in God's timing he will become a Christian.

Though there is much speculation about the timing of Jesus' return, there are two aspects about the future that scripture makes certain. The first is that when Jesus returns he will come as the King to rule his Kingdom. The second is that he will return as a Bridegroom to claim his bride (the body of all true believers). Both of these certainties should call us to pray and work towards the restoration of God's Kingdom in our area(s) of influence, whether at local, national or international level. Though we recognise nothing will ever be perfect until Jesus returns, we are, in the meantime, called to undertake our Father's business.

> It's not just any work, it's the work he has sent us to do in partnership with him.

He is our boss and we get to be his apprentice, learning and developing. This is the best apprenticeship scheme available to the human race and the good news is that we are uniquely qualified as his son or daughter to be hired. We have an opportunity to shift from limiting God's Kingdom by being the dam, to becoming the river that flows with all that the Kingdom has to offer to bring about a reformation.

This is not a question of looking busy for when Jesus returns, but actively playing your part – across all the areas of influence – in preparing society for when he comes for his bride.

I have an incredible friend who is achieving this in education. His journey outlines how walking from a Kingdom perspective can make a difference:

After completing a music degree and, not knowing what to do next, I embarked on a teacher training course. It was then that I heard God's call and the buzz and excitement of 'making a difference' in the classroom. As my career evolved I was promoted to headteacher of an extremely challenging mixed comprehensive school in North London. Over the years my journey was like a roller-coaster – highs, lows, loads of prayer and lots of adrenalin! The transformation was striking as teaching and learning became the heart of the school with the curriculum more relevant to the students' needs and aspirations. Data was used more powerfully to track progress and engage parents in helping all the students succeed. The school environment was improved and all the children felt safer, happier and were immensely proud of their school with a desire to learn. Outcomes massively improved with Ofsted rating the school as 'Outstanding'.

God's hand was definitely involved. Staff made comments such as 'It is like a cloud has been lifted from the place' and 'I can't believe the difference one person can make'. I was reminded that with God all things are possible and it was great to passionately lead and transform a school along godly principles, seriously increasing the life chances for thousands of students. I now oversee a dynamic and exciting Multi-academy Trust and I have the privilege of working alongside other inspiring and dedicated teachers and leaders. Every day I have the opportunity to speak positively to staff and students in a godly way that makes a difference to their lives and shapes education in the local area in a strategic way. God has had a huge influence throughout my career. He has opened so many doors for me as a Lead Strategic Partner in teaching and learning partnerships and consortiums, serving on school forums and at a regional and national level on various educational management committees. I am invited to speak at regional and national conferences about school culture, systems and transformational leadership. I have had the opportunity to showcase work with a number of local, national and international partners, including schools and universities across Europe and America.

Amidst all of this, however, it is still the kind word, the thoughtful deed, the servant-hearted leadership, the value that I place on others, the remembering of a student's name and the praise and recognition of goodness in their lives that makes the job that I do so inspiring and effective. Whatever job you have, you will have relationships with people around you and you will have a level of influence. When we can fully understand the importance of being filled on a daily basis with the Holy Spirit and that we are sons and daughters of an awesome heavenly King and walk standing 10-feet tall because we know that we are loved by a heavenly Father and that he has placed eternity in our heart, given us access to the power, the wisdom and the authority of heaven and the ability to love others as Jesus loved us, then we will have an immense impact. In other words, ordinary things will become extraordinary. Remember you are a prince or princess of God and people adore princes and princesses. They watch their every move, they want to be like them and, by bringing this presence into their midst, you will have great influence and bring great hope.

Goals

Our first goal is to allow the Holy Spirit to continue to define our character and behaviour as the holy bride without spot or blemish, as we go about our 'works'. In Galatians 5:22–23 we read that the fruit of the Spirit is Love, Joy, Peace, Forbearance, Kindness, Goodness, Faithfulness, Gentleness and Self-control. God delights as we grow in the fruits of the Spirit because he can use us more powerfully when our character outstrips our gifts. Growing in character is not about our public persona but living a lifestyle of integrity and holiness before God, including when no one is looking. It flows from the decisions we make and how we choose to behave in our pursuit of God 24/7. Nothing changes us more than spending time with God because,

> whatever the problem or situation he is always the answer.

Separate from God we can do nothing but, as we grow in character, keeping our eyes fixed on Jesus and declaring his will over people and situations, his love and compassion flow through us.

Our second goal needs to be to establish the culture of God's Kingdom in our area(s) of influence by considering the question 'What might it look like in heaven?' We can best achieve this by inviting the Holy Spirit to dwell in us every day and guide us as we go about our daily activities.

Keeping ourselves aligned with these two goals of character and Kingdom will be essential if you are to navigate through the difficult and turbulent times in the years ahead. Ultimately, this is about the spiritual and cultural legacy our generation will leave for the next as that final day comes ever closer and Jesus returns to earth. I love the moment in the film *The Lion King*[12] when Mufasa the lion shows his cub Simba the Kingdom that is to be his inheritance. It stretches as far as he can see. We also have an incredible Kingdom to inherit because of our relationship with Jesus. Let's recognise the enormity of our inheritance as royal sons and daughters and roar our intent so that God's Kingdom will come 'on earth as it is in heaven'. Let's not waste our opportunity to change the Christian landscape to one that is about outwardly reflecting the character of God and influencing society around us from the Kingdom perspective.

Discussion and Activation

Which aspects of Kingdom have you previously identified with and which have you not considered to pray for 'on earth as it is in heaven' (Salvation and Healing, Freedom (Deliverance), Peace, Joy, Justice (Righteousness), God's Presence and his Comfort)?

What might your area(s) of influence look like in heaven and how can you bring this on earth?

In your area(s) of influence, if you are the first Bible that someone 'reads', what impression will they get about Jesus? How will people around you catch a glimpse of the Father's love?

In what ways (i.e. integrity, holiness and the fruits of the Spirit), are you allowing the Holy Spirit to touch your heart and define your character?

6
How to Influence: Military Manoeuvres

We live in such unprecedented times, with things moving so fast across the world and all areas of society. God is literally shaking all of us to bring an unshakable Kingdom, spiritually, physically and financially. Now is the time for the Church to radically obey the call on our lives to make history and transform the world to reflect God's Kingdom. Every believer is called to make disciples wherever God places them, and the areas of influence, through the presence of the Holy Spirit, are where the Kingdom can so magnificently strike back. Whichever area(s) you are called to influence,

> it's time to step up and step out.

What is exciting is that many church leaders are recognising the need to raise disciples and release their church communities, both men and women, to occupy all the areas of influence: arts, business, church, distribution of media, education, family and community, government, healthcare and so on – we all have the God-given authority to bring about cultural transformation. Let's not measure our success by how many people gather on Sunday but rather by how many positively impact on the world. To be blunt, what is now required is a complete paradigm shift in church thinking from people inwardly serving church leaders, to church leaders actively encouraging their communities to position themselves outwardly giving support wherever it is required, as illustrated below in the diagram of serving models.

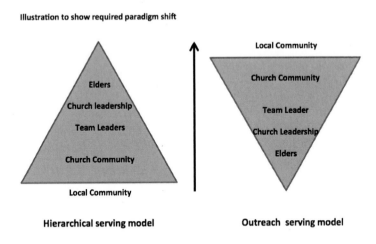

Illustration to show required paradigm shift

Hierarchical serving model   Outreach serving model

We often pray for elders and church leaders but how often do we reach out to workplace leaders so that they feel the unity, support and collaboration from their Christian family? Each and every one of us has a significant role to play but, in particular, apostolic and prophetic leaders who act as gatekeepers into various areas of influence have a prominent role in leading the way and transforming society around us. We need to encourage influential gatekeepers in the other areas of influence as they hold the keys to unlock their workplace and transform society. A tiger is only powerful in its own environment and should not be placed in captivity in a cage, believing a lie that you can only serve God in full-time church ministry. Let's become excellent in the way we encourage and raise our workplace leaders. Let's provide biblical, Kingdom-leadership training that fully equips leaders instead of leaving them trying to bring together lessons they have learnt in church with the secular teaching provided by business schools and workplace development programmes.

As I shift from the mindset that church is about Sunday, a building and the people, I am recognising that church is happening in my place of work as I run leadership programmes and coach managers. I love the opportunities God opens up to raise disciples under the umbrella of leadership and organisational development.

One of my clients wanted to more fully understand herself and explore the question 'What makes a good leader?' As we began to explore her leadership style I felt God talk to me about the need for my client to 'lighten up and grow down'. He wanted to restore joy that had been stripped from her during childhood so that it would permeate all her relationships, whether personal or those at work. Sharing with her that I sensed maybe joy had been lost in her childhood, this struck a chord with her and she announced that she was a Christian, with the words 'the joy of the Lord is my strength'. Feeling the presence of the Holy Spirit in the room I declared over her that joy be restored into every aspect of her life, and that the particular year would become a year of abundant joy. Over the following coaching sessions her identity as a daughter of the King increased as the lies of Satan dissipated and Peace and Joy began to flow more freely. It was amazing to see her transformation. But God is so kind he did not want to stop there. He opened the door to allow her to realise that she is not only adopted but an ambassador of heaven with the power to bring Kingdom into her workplace. No one had explained this before but from that moment a Kingdom princess was released into the business area of influence. Now, her daily 'work' activities include prayer and Kingdom declarations as she walks around the office, and she is able to spend time worshipping Jesus as she listens to music for worship (through her headphones) whilst she works. It makes me smile to think that she is walking in her true identity and destiny, bringing a Kingdom approach to work in a way that glorifies God.

As Christians we have access to the Father and there is never a moment when he does not want to talk and share his heart with us. Through this relationship he loves to reveal himself and the prophetic is one way that he encourages, comforts, builds up and loves people.

Having met my husband 30 years ago, the more time we spend together the easier it has become to recognise his voice and understand his heart and his way of thinking. In the same way we need to learn how to tune in to God's frequency, to recognise and respond to his voice and heart. If this is new to you, start by seeking to understand how God connects with you. How do you hear, see or sense his presence? Do you hear his voice talking to you inside your head that may be a prophecy or word of knowledge for you or someone else? Does he give you pictures, like a photo or little movie playing out in your head? Don't dismiss random thoughts that suddenly come into your thinking, a dream that you have or a picture or impression that appears in your mind. Sometimes even objects 'say' things to you, at other times you may see a word over someone. What revelation is he imparting? Ask God what it means and what he would like you to do with what he has shared with you? Don't feel you have to blurt out immediately what you are hearing, seeing or sensing but learn to chew on it, like chewing a toffee, so that you can experience the full flavour. As you do so, allow God to share not just your revelation but the interpretation and application for the person or situation.

> True prophetic ministry is looking for the gold
> in the midst of the dirt in people's lives.

We need to learn how to connect with God's love for each individual, to allow him to share his heart with the individual. The goal of prophecy is to encourage and build not confuse, control or manipulate and it is important to weigh the prophetic against God's truth in the Bible. This is just a snapshot on how to hear God. (There are many great books that can help you understand the prophetic, a few of which are listed in 'Further Reading' at the end of this book.) The prophetic gift is one we should all desire, ask for and receive as soon as we give our lives to Christ.

> I have one client who gave her life to Jesus and over the following month immediately began to have encounters with God as he began to highlight his truths to her. Driving her car whilst listening to the radio, it suddenly tuned out and, as she went to adjust the tuning, the words 'don't worry' appeared on the radio panel – not once but twice. She went on to share with me that she had had a pair of jeans for two years but only just noticed that the brand was 'amazing woman'. Excitedly she asked, 'Is this God speaking to me?' As she seeks him more and more, her prophetic gift will develop and that will impact on the people she influences in her workplace.

When I am with clients I often sense the nudge of the Holy Spirit bringing what God has shared with me, whether it is a picture or words, in secular language. You don't have to be freaky when these opportunities occur; act normally as you receive the revelation. No bashing people around the head with the Bible but expressing the Bible by showing the love of Jesus. His love is so irresistible people can't help but be attracted to him. The trick is to be obedient to the Holy Spirit but honour the person and where they currently are. At the end of the encounter the priority is for the person to feel loved and cared for above anything else that happens.

One gentleman I coached had been raised as a Muslim, which provided a number of opportunities to share our perspectives on the enormity of God's Creation and his power. At his second-to-last session a window of opportunity opened through God sharing a word of knowledge with me about this man's relationship with his dad and how Father God had something very different to offer; that he is not a distant, angry Dad but one that is slow to anger and full of unconditional love for him as his beloved son. We had a great discussion whilst respecting the journey of faith the gentleman was travelling.

As well as loving the person, remember that we don't encourage and prophesy in the hope of victory, but do so from a place of hope and from a place of victory that Jesus has already won for us through his resurrection. Let's position ourselves from that place of victory and the abundant love that Jesus has for us and for each individual we encounter. We live in the glorious revelation of the Kingdom being available to us, even though we may not experience all that it is today, tomorrow or the day after. Manage the tension of the now but possibly not yet when you prophesy in part or see healings but accept that not everyone gets healed. God does not owe us an explanation as to why this happens but he does ask his followers to be expectant and respond through trusting their relationship with him. Though we may not see the fullness, go after it 'as if' (i.e. the expectation is not unfounded) because that is what God desires – celebrate together each moment along the way. Keep humble, keep expectant, keep connected and keep trusting the Father. This is part of the mystery of God and his sovereignty reigns over us. The more we learn to tune in and respond the more likely we are to grow in the gifts of the Spirit, prophesying more and more accurately over people and seeing people healed and restored.

Covert Operations (the Undercover Mission)

Increasingly I am realising that bringing the Kingdom to earth is about covert as well as overt operations and we need to learn how to discern with the Holy Spirit which way to go. My battle strategy is to continuously recognise the little things that covertly reflect God's Kingdom. This may be random acts of kindness such as flowers left for someone I can see is struggling or just encouraging a receptionist as I arrive at a client's office. Everyone likes encouragement and from this place often the prophetic will flow!

> I arrived at a client's building and went to the little kitchen area to make myself a coffee before starting a day of coaching. I noticed a Muslim lady who had just finished her shift as a cleaner and I started to thank her for doing her job so well, encouraging her in realising her important role within the business. As I did this she beamed and was obviously quite taken aback. Sadly, encouragement was not what she usually experienced but I was simply valuing her and bringing a bit of heaven here on earth.

Maybe today is an opportunity to encourage those who so often are in the background doing a good job: cleaners, receptionists, waiters, canteen assistants, delivery people, parking attendants and playground supervisors are just a few examples; there are many who do unseen jobs that benefit us all and keep us safe. These opportunities are all around, so be intentional in recognising and taking action as you spot them.

We are called to be 'salt and light' (Matthew 5:13–16) but need to do this using everyday language that people relate to. 'Thou say'st the Lord', puts people off; instead, engage and articulate it in a way they can understand.

I was asked to carry out a one-off leadership feedback session with a manager. As we started to explore the first pages of his latest appraisal report I felt God share with me that despite the report being good the gentleman believed himself to be a fraud. Recently appointed as a manager and lacking in confidence he was walking in daily fear of being found out. So, using covert language, I simply said, 'Listening to you, I just get the sense that you believe you are incapable of a managerial role, like there is a little chatterbox voice saying you are a fraud and this makes you fearful that you will fail.' Bingo! I was able to say that this was a lie, rebuked the lie (in my head, declaring in Jesus' name) and declared truth over him by pulling out particular phrases in the report that I felt God was highlighting to illustrate his strengths. That young man walked out with his head held high feeling very different about himself and his capabilities. He encountered the love of Jesus without realising it.

Often covert operations lead to overt opportunities because the individual catches a glimpse of Jesus and likes what they see, feel and hear. Sometimes you don't have to work too hard to do this.

On one such occasion one client announced that he did not just need to learn about emotional intelligence but also spiritual intelligence. This was clearly a divine appointment orchestrated by God to bring the two of us together. I had the privilege of leading him through repentance and Deliverance from his unhealthy involvement in a spiritualist church, led him to Christ and witnessed him filled by the Holy Spirit, all in a two-hour, one-to-one coaching session.

My start point is that any client I coach has been sent to me by God, so I begin a dialogue with him around how I might help?

I go with my gut feeling and pray into this, storing up weaponry in preparation for when we actually meet. Before clients arrive, I take any opportunity I can to prayer walk the room and carry out prophetic actions as a way of bringing God's Kingdom down to earth. Such actions may simply be to brush off what I am sensing from a chair or even stand on a chair and take authority over what I am sensing (yes, I know that sounds a little crazy but it does work!). It is important to recognise that the power of prayer and praying can change the atmosphere around an individual or situation.

I also factor in that God's timing is perfect so not only has someone been 'sent' to me but this is exactly the moment in time that we are destined to meet.

Whilst coaching one client, she and I were exploring the area of emotional intelligence and God gave me a word of knowledge that I translated into secular language around 'I sense that as a child you were treated like Cinderella, always serving the rest of the family and you never went to the ball. I believe that it is time for you to go to the ball.' As one of the youngest of 12 children, this was her experience and the covert wording opened a door to a whole new conversation. The weekend before she'd been to a charity ball and won an iPad, exclaiming, 'I never win anything.' This made me smile as I recognised God partnering with me in the discussion with her that she could have good stuff and she is worth it! Several months later she let me know that this new perspective had made such a difference. She had stopped trying to mother everyone and control everything and, in her own words, is now 'living as if I am on a light, happy cloud'.

It radically changed how she leads her team and how she deals with her personal relationships. She experienced something of the Father's love and goodness without realising.

I seek to reflect the Christian message using secular language not just in one-to-one coaching situations but also when facilitating leadership development programmes. An example is the module I teach around 'Leading Through Conflict'. I am teaching directly from the Bible, as given in Matthew 18:15, but I use secular words along the lines of: 'Go to the person and, in private, talk through the issue openly and authentically with the aim of reconciliation', no gossip or slander, and no seeking allies, which can escalate into open warfare. I then make the link to working collaboratively through the culture of honour.

One of my favourite Bible passages is Isaiah 60:1–3: *'Arise, shine, for your light has come, and the glory of the LORD rises upon you. See, darkness covers the earth and thick darkness is over the peoples, but the LORD rises upon you and his glory appears over you. Nations will come to your light, and kings to the brightness of your dawn.'* Such powerful words ignite something in me to want to bring God's presence and light where there is darkness, even in undercover, covert scenarios. In doing this, our Saviour is glorified. You may question such a hidden approach because surely we are called to make Jesus known and see salvation but this comes back to our mission to transform society. What I do know is that having caught sight of God's Kingdom, people go on to ask questions and this has led to several people giving their lives to Christ just by my walking with them, initially from a covert place. Covert operations are all about sowing seeds that create a Kingdom perspective. Our goal is to love people, let them glimpse Jesus and he will save them when the time is right.

Overt Operations (Revealing God's Presence)

Together with everyday covert operations, I also try to recognise the overt moments when the Holy Spirit delivers an opportunity to pray, prophesy or share the gospel. It is about being sensitive to the presence of God. This is often through words of knowledge or just a sense that I get, a random or nagging thought that will not go away. I recognise this is God's way of bringing someone out of a place that they've been locked, through sin or various hurts, habits and hang-ups used by Satan to bring ungodly lies or sickness – body and soul. This is the way God desires to partner with us, whether we are at church or in our workplace, and when he speaks he releases the power to back-up what you and I are giving. God is waiting for us to have an open heart and to hear him.

> During another coaching session I felt God say, 'Be open about your faith.' So, as I was explaining about the chatterbox voice that broadcasts in our minds all the negative things, I added that as a practising Christian I recognise these to be lies from Satan. The client became tearful exclaiming that the week before she had prayed to God to send her a Christian coach! Being able to coach and prophesy openly over the following sessions was wonderful.

I used to think that 'ministry' was a very serious, sombre experience and you can buy into the lie that ministry is a heavy burden that we carry, but more and more I am realising it does not have to be like that. When I was a young child my dad always carried my dance or school bag leaving me free to hold his hand and skip along happily beside him. As God's beloved daughter, I get to have fun working with him every day without having to carry the weight and burdens of the world on my shoulders – that's his job. There are times when the Holy Spirit is doing deep work in someone's heart that requires great sensitivity and after these encounters I am intentional around 'brushing off' anything that has been shared so that I do not carry anything away that is not mine. Generally, though, most encounters are more light-hearted and fun, but with a serious punch behind them.

At another coaching session God gave me a word of knowledge around 'called to be an inventor', which started as a covert conversation that quickly led to the client asking, 'How do you know that?' I told him, 'I am a Christian who believes God speaks today and God shared this with me to encourage you.' This led to a very brief discussion about the gospel. At his final coaching session a few months later, over snacks he had arranged, he began by initiating a conversation with, 'This is like our last supper.' He went on to share that he had been researching a little bit about Christianity and had come across a secular song, which he had printed for me to read. The words that had resonated for him were about knowing Jesus and reaching out to him because he cares and hears your prayers.   The lyrics led to a very overt conversation which finished with me doing a prophetic dream interpretation, not just for him but later with a graduate he mentors, which took place in the middle of the workplace canteen! A moment of open heaven here on earth when Father God revealed his love!

Like a soldier in battle, be open to carry out both covert as well as overt operations and have some fun with God along the way. Our posture around...

> supernatural events must not become divorced from our everyday life

...separating the sacred from the secular. People are interested in the supernatural and seek to understand it because most have no terms of reference to work out what they have seen, heard or sensed. I'm often asked to explain what clients are experiencing supernaturally, some of which is good because it is from God and some which is not so good because it is from Satan. Both opportunities excite me because everything from God is totally good but when you can bring Satan's schemes into the light they no longer have such a hold. Satan's opportunity is over once we go on the offensive to bring God's truth and goodness into that situation. As we recognise any supposed coincidence could be an opportunity from God, understand what God is saying or doing before the moment passes. Be ready to follow his footsteps as he draws people closer to him. Love them and in so doing seek to draw them closer to the one who will save. Through covert and overt operations help those around you to make sense of their spiritual journey and in so doing God will reveal his heart directly to them.

Discussion and Activation

How actively do you partner with God in your area(s) of influence? Do you take the time to talk to him about what's happening? Do you listen to his answers to your questions and act on what he shares?

How might you develop your ability to influence through covert and overt opportunities?

Start to journal your stories to build your faith. These will both encourage and help you to be intentional around covert and overt opportunities. I find this very helpful and it's great to reread all that God has done.

7
How to Influence: Partnering with the Holy Spirit and Others

Whether covert or overt operations, both require us to partner with the Holy Spirit and actively discern with him how to approach people and situations. On a day-to-day basis, Jesus lived with his feet on the ground focused on the Father's mission, his heart relationally connected to people whilst thinking 'upwards' towards his Father in heaven. He modelled for us a lifestyle of being present with God rather than giving him Sunday and occasional weekday visitation rights or a quick prayer at the end of the day.

> God's desire is to partner with us at all times

...at church, our workplace or wherever we find ourselves. God is waiting for his people to have a relationship with him 24/7. He loves to reveal his heart for all his children, whether they know him or not, and the Holy Spirit loves to express his love through us. The amazing thing to grasp is that when God speaks he releases the power to back up what we are releasing, which means we can expect and take on great things from God. We need to be full of confidence in him knowing God will give us all we need. This is about learning to connect with his reality, which becomes our everyday supernatural life.

On one occasion, I had arrived early at a client's building and was sitting in reception having a quiet chat with God when someone I had previously coached walked in looking really unwell. I encouraged him to come and sit with me despite his protests because he had a heavy cold, was beginning to ache all over and did not want to pass on the infection. Discovering what was wrong I offered to pray with him, just a quick prayer for 'all flu symptoms to go in Jesus' name'. Immediately he felt hot all over but a little better and off he went looking slightly bewildered. Ten minutes later he reappeared still feeling 'weird' but much better and exclaimed, 'I don't know what is happening to me,' to which I responded, 'It's Jesus,' which made him smile. I happened to see one of his colleagues two weeks later who told me that the day after I had prayed all his flu symptoms had completely gone.

The more we allow the Holy Spirit to lead, the easier it is for God to develop us. There is, however, an important point that I want to emphasise: partnering with the Holy Spirit is about pursuing the person of God, his presence and glory, not just his power.

> We can so easily fall into the trap of seeing the
> Holy Spirit as our supernatural butler

...who fetches and carries for us rather than our best friend who we love and want to be with. Intimacy with the Father always comes before the Great Commission. We must go beyond the manifestations and seek his revelation because when we experience the manifest glory of God – his love, goodness and inner beauty – that's when his mighty power comes to us. Experiencing God's glory in this way is not about his power but his love. We need to be in love with Jesus for who he is not just what he can do for us. Moving in spiritual power is a by-product not an end-product of what we truly desire, which is an intimate relationship with God; to be his closest friend, we need to want to get to know him and desire encounters in partnership with him as we live our lives together. We need to walk with Jesus in the same way he walked with his Father throughout his ministry, knowing his affirmation as a beloved son and from a place of approval. From the promptings of his Father, Jesus took every opportunity to teach, to prophesy, to heal and raise the dead. I like the reality of being an ambassador for the Kingdom on a mission throughout the day. Covert or overt I love how our storylines unfold as we continue to walk and share intimacy with God.

A few years ago I was invited to attend an institution's summer party. I could feel the negative atmosphere caused by 'having to prove yourself' and approached each conversation as an opportunity to input a piece of heaven, looking to shift the atmosphere covertly through encouragement, acceptance and kindness. These encounters opened the door to being invited to give a talk at one of the institute's training evenings on a subject of my choice. So I asked God what he wanted from me and he gave me a title: 'courageous leadership' (covered in a later chapter). Within this talk I included a top tip on 'spiritual sensitivity that is louder than popular opinion'. This was all about not leaving your spirituality at the door and so allowing trends, popular opinion or a louder voice in the workplace to hold sway over what you truly know and believe in your heart, because they are inseparable. Interestingly, after the talk it was this particular point people wanted to discuss. As I stood with a glass of wine in one hand and a canapé in the other, one particular lady asked, 'What happens if you have no spirituality?' I heard God rephrase this into a question to ask her: 'Why do you think you have no spirituality?' This led into a conversation that, as a young child in a Catholic convent school, she had been told by one of the nuns that she lacked faith. This gave a beautiful opportunity to overtly share the truth of the gospel message around relationship and the Father's unconditional love for her.

Perseverance and Handling Disappointment

My testimonies might sound as though I find these opportunities easy and that conversations never go pear-shaped but in reality I don't and I often get things wrong.

I recently found myself with half an hour to spare and asked God if there was someone in the coffee shop I could encourage. I felt that God gave me a word of knowledge about a challenging presentation the gentleman next to me was giving that afternoon and to encourage him to stand on his convictions despite any opposition he would face in the room. When I shared this he replied that it did not resonate and obviously did not want to talk, which left an awkward silence as I gulped down of my coffee so that I could make my hasty exit. By God's grace I step out in obedience and faith; he always covers the situation and smiles over me. Whether I get the prophetic revelation, interpretation and application right or wrong and whether the individual receives or rejects what I bring,

> God's measurement of success is about giving it a go,
> taking the risk and, as you do so, loving the person.

I can assure you there are many people who travel the London

Underground who think I am some sort of madwoman but I would rather be a fool for God than miss an opportunity. It bugs me far more if I don't have the courage of my convictions than if I step out and get rejected, because I wonder what that opportunity to be courageous might have revealed. At times when I feel really challenged by people's attitudes and behaviours around me, I seek God's reassurance and take a minute to shelter under his wing. I can easily feel like I am on an escalator travelling in the opposite direction to everyone else but God is my comfort and reminds me that, although it feels like I am going against the tide, I am actually moving the right way when others aren't. This encourages me to keep my eyes fixed on him, receiving his unconditional love, and seeing things from heaven's perspective. Covert and overt operations are not for our own gratification to make us feel good as we seek to hear a 'well done'. Hearing God's love for people is a privilege, and the more time we spend with the Holy Spirit the more our overwhelming desire to love people overflows. The power of encouragement and the ability to communicate prophetically is for all Christians not just an elite few. You just need to,

> have the courage to take yourselves beyond your self-inflicted limitations

...that are usually driven by fear of humiliation and public embarrassment. Do not partner with the wrong attitude but instead step out in obedience to what you are feeling and sensing from the Holy Spirit and make the choice to partner with him. Remember, *'For the Spirit God gave us does not make us timid, but gives us power, love and self-discipline'* (2 Timothy 1:7). Develop self-discipline, become conscious of God's presence over any challenging situation and do not link up with anything that takes you away from him. When you face a problem or impossible situation, learn to laugh at it rather than allow the problem to become bigger than your awareness of God, his love, power and presence.

Although we look to Jesus as our role model, the reality is that we will not always get it right or people will not always respond in the way we hoped. The danger of disappointment is that it can lead us into questioning God's character and our identity in him, which attacks our godly expectations. Disappointment does not cancel our assignment or God's presence but it does build a wall that blocks our view of the horizon, creating a barrier between us and God. As the brick wall goes up it attacks our courage to step out. Satan uses disappointment to lie and rob us of our future and we empower him by agreeing with his deception. It calls into question our identity, buying into various lies around 'I must have done something wrong'. Faith is about belief and expectation but if we allow disappointment to accumulate this significantly reduces our expectation of God's love, goodness and power. We need to stay in the place of God's grace and love and learn how to effectively process our disappointment with him. There have been many occasions when I have had an incredible experience in a coaching session when God has clearly spoken to me about a client and I have overtly shared with that individual something of God's heart for them. At the next session, if there is no reference to last time's discussion and because I have not felt prompted by the Holy Spirit, I don't follow up. In these moments I have to make a choice to not take offence with God but continue to trust him and carry on with his agenda for that person. Whilst I have had the privilege of sowing some seeds, their salvation or breakthrough will come at another time or through someone else. It is a sobering reminder that life is not about me but about God's will and his relationship with that person. The truth is that God is always good and always works for our good and the good of others. Stand up for truth and keep your heart soft to his goodness so that he can continue to work with you.

We live in an instant, fast-track, microwave-riddled world and like to see immediate results. When we don't, there is a danger we will take control and seek our alternative solutions because we wrongly think we know better than God. We stop partnering with the Holy Spirit and start our own quest, which is foolish, dangerous and a waste of time and energy. The result can be our own Israelite-like version of walking into the wilderness rather than keeping on track towards our promised land. Don't start to be critical or judgemental because things have not gone 'your way' because this simply holds you captive. Instead, rest in your secret place with God, receiving his love and affection, and there store up positive weaponry to use in the future when the time is right. So often, by keeping in close relationship with God, I have sensed his love simply for stepping out and being obedient, concluding that I am on track even if it does not feel that way. The truth is that God is with us in all circumstances and, as Job 19:25 declares, *'I know that my redeemer lives, and that in the end he will stand on the earth.'* For many years I have kept testimony cards, rather like truth cards but recording a summary of my encounters with people, that reflect all that God has done through my ministry. They help to keep me on track, reminding me that God is an incredible, loving, generous, spontaneous, orderly, ever-present and forever-good God. Remembering who he is and staying in a place of worship and thanksgiving keeps our heart focused on him rather than any prowling deception of Satan.

Don't Travel Alone

As we gathered people within various areas of influence at my local church, a common theme emerged: a feeling of isolation against a secular tide that can feel overwhelming. Thankfully, we live under the new covenant and are not meant to operate as lone apostles, prophets, teachers, evangelists and pastors. I am learning more and more the power of working in teams, with supportive, like-minded people around me. The workplace can feel dominated by a sense of individualisation, isolation, performance, entitlement and fear but we are lucky to have Christian family around us who will support, encourage, challenge and provide a much-needed Kingdom perspective.

Several years ago at my local church we began King's Business – a workplace community comprising small to large business owners, freelance consultants and people who work corporately. King's Business plays a key role in preventing a feeling of isolation; it is like a hub of hope where we can find support, encouragement and develop healthy relationships with other like-minded Christians. There is also teaching on the Kingdom of Heaven that equips us for our 'works' and a place to share stories and testimonies. This is what one of our members has to say about being a part of King's Business:

'I started my own business seven years ago. Since it involved consulting in a specialist area, I felt that local business networks were of limited help to me. A friend suggested that I visit a King's Business breakfast at a local church and I found it incredibly refreshing. Instead of focusing on running a business I realised we are called to bring a positive godly influence and it was an encouragement to me to intentionally bring the Kingdom of God into my work. I became a regular at the breakfasts and found people there who would challenge me in my personal walk with the Father, pray for me and speak God's words to me. Such a "business network" has been a significant encouragement and led me to stand in a food production factory asking God what he wants to say to help with the problem or to speak to those around me. Every job I take becomes an opportunity for the Father to change the atmosphere. Belonging to the King's Business community maintains my focus on God and his purposes, rather than depending on my own strength. In turn, I am able to encourage others in the community in their pursuit of the Kingdom in their work.'

I also belong to a Christian business network that meets in Central London, which enables me to meet many like-minded Christians who also see their workplace as the place to influence.[13] I encourage you to find others in your church environment and also in your place of work who you can partner with. Don't travel alone! Let's be family together, reaching out to others within our church community, other churches and like-minded fellow travellers locally, nationally and internationally, to enable us to impact all the areas of influence.

The story of Saul's conversion on the road to Damascus (Acts 9:1–20), is a wonderful example of how we can encounter God's glory, power and presence in everyday life. In such moments God can do anything: heal the sick, set people free, even raise the dead. Having met Jesus on the road to Damascus, Saul's life was forever changed and his transformation began, from persecutor to one of the most influential Christians in history. God as Creator and King can do all things and yet, out of his love for us and his desire for a relationship with his children, chooses to partner with you and me, giving us the opportunity to do even greater things than Jesus did during his time on earth. The question is,

> are we receptive and willing to partner with God
> as we meet and travel alongside others on their road to Damascus?

Let's not miss this incredible opportunity to go on covert and overt military manoeuvres in partnership with the Holy Spirit and fellow Christians and together bring God's Kingdom and cultural transformation wherever we go.

Discussion and Activation

How can you become better at discerning what the Holy Spirit is doing or saying?

How good are you at processing disappointment and does this impact your ability to reach out to others?

Who are the Saul-type characters in your area(s) of influence that God is speaking to you about? How can you love them and bring Kingdom to them?

8
How to Influence: As a Kingdom-Style Leader

Having redefined the way we see work, identified our area(s) of influence and explored how to partner with the Holy Spirit from a Kingdom perspective through covert or overt operations, let's now focus on how to influence in a way that is becoming to our role as ambassadors of heaven.

People who marry into royal circles go through a process of preparation for public life prior to taking on their official duties. Similarly, as the bride of Christ and recognising our royal inheritance, God seeks to prepare us for service so that we are recognisable as co-heirs in Christ and ambassadors for the Kingdom of Heaven. If we allow him, God's desire is to develop our character and shape our thinking and behaviour to one that reflects him.

The Jewish people waited hundreds of years for their King to turn up and rescue them. Isaiah prophesied: *'For to us a child is born, to us a son is given, and the government will be on his shoulders. And he will be called Wonderful Counsellor, Mighty God, Everlasting Father, Prince of Peace'* (Isaiah 9:6). Sadly, because Jesus did not appear riding an impressive chariot, wearing a crown and brandishing a sword as he led a massive fighting army, most failed to notice his arrival. Jesus may not have looked like their image of a king but, throughout his ministry, he exemplified royal Kingdom leadership as he went about his daily activities, mentoring the disciples, teaching the people, healing the sick, freeing the opposed and raising the dead.

Taking Jesus as the example, what are the qualities that make a Kingdom-style leader stand out from the crowd, whether they are a formal leader or not? Importantly, as we have already explored, they are rooted in their identity as a child of God and everything flows from intimately knowing who they are and who they are loved by. Their thoughts and actions grow from a deep trust that Father God is the ultimate provider and protector who prevents them from falling into the trap of seeking approval and favour elsewhere.

They are also visionary and hope-filled in the way they lead – seeing things from an eternal perspective and knowing God as Creator and Ruler over everything.

Kingdom-style leaders know how to handle their own power and prosperity so that they can be a godly influence in their area(s) of influence. Abraham Lincoln famously said, 'Nearly all men can stand adversity, but if you want to test a man's character, give him power.' A good leader never uses power to humiliate or manipulate but, instead, encourages and supports people. They understand that,

> any position of power increases the importance to keep leaning on God, to trust him and continue to rely on him.

They prioritise a lifestyle of prayer and intimacy with God because they realise that any power bestowed is a test of their character.

A true Kingdom-style leader will see leadership as a privilege and any power given to them provides a platform to serve; it's the opportunity to remain humble and lift others up.

Kingdom-style leaders project the fruits of the Spirit listed in Galatians 5:22–23: Love, Joy, Peace, Forbearance, Kindness,

Goodness, Faithfulness, Gentleness, Self-control. Verse 23 goes on to say that *'against such things there is no law'*. They express the fruits of the Spirit in the way they work, collaborate with and honour everyone they serve, guide and bring wise counsel. Such character and behaviour distinguishes them as men and women of Peace. They also display incredible emotional maturity, building healthy relationships and galvanising those around them towards a shared vision.

Kingdom-style leaders understand that as believers they have been given the gift of the Holy Spirit. It was Jesus himself who emphasised the importance of receiving the Holy Spirit, telling the disciples in Acts 1:4–5: *'Do not leave Jerusalem, but wait for the gift my Father promised, which you have heard me speak about. For John baptised with water, but in a few days you will be baptised with the Holy Spirit.'* He then goes on to say in Acts 1:8, *'You will receive power when the Holy Spirit comes on you; and you will be my witnesses in Jerusalem, and in all Judea and Samaria, and to the ends of the earth.'* And in Acts 2:38–39 Peter reinforces Christ's message when he addresses the crowd declaring: *'Repent and be baptised, every one of you, in the name of Jesus Christ for the forgiveness of your sins. And you will receive the gift of the Holy Spirit. The promise is for you and your children and for all who are far off – for all whom the Lord our God will call.'* A Kingdom-style leader understands the importance of constantly being filled with the Holy Spirit in order to be effective as God's witness in their area(s) of influence, whether locally, nationally or internationally. Jesus made it possible for us to receive the Holy Spirit by going to the Father, declaring to us through the power of the Holy Spirit that we would do even greater things than he achieved during his time on earth. In 1 Corinthians 14:1 the apostle Paul writes that we should *'eagerly desire gifts of the Spirit, especially prophecy'*. Such gifts include wisdom, knowledge, faith, healing, working of miracles, prophecy, discerning of spirits, speaking in and the interpretation of tongues. Such gifts are freely given by God and are separate from any inherent capabilities that we have, so that we do not fall into the trap of pride and boasting about them. From their place of identity Kingdom-style leaders live within the reality that the Kingdom of God is on hand and, powered by the constant filling of the Holy Spirit, seek to use these gifts in a way that exalts Christ, witnessing God's love and power that brings transformation to society around them. Through their actions, Jesus brings the lost into his Kingdom and the Church grows in numbers.

Kingdom-style leaders are fiercely courageous and optimistic as they go about their mission, living naturally 'supernatural' lifestyles – praying for the sick, raising the dead, prophesying over people and bringing Kingdom wherever they go.

In partnership with the Holy Spirit, they not only effectively discern people and situations, they make the choice to take authority over any negative atmosphere and, in doing so, bring what it is affecting into alignment with heaven. They are a force to be reckoned with that makes Satan quake because he has nothing in his armoury to stop them when they are totally focused on who they are and their mission to *'Go and make disciples...'*

Through love and compassion for others it's important we walk in the same way as Jesus, declaring through our words and actions, *'Our Father in heaven, hallowed be your name, your kingdom come, your will be done, on earth as it is in heaven'* (Matthew 6:9–10).

> Kingdom-style leaders seek to transform culture not just survive it

...and as they do so, raise-up people around them to do the same. *'You will shine among them like stars in the sky as you hold firmly to the word of life*' (Philippians 2:15–16). Every Christian is called to join Jesus' Great Commission and our greatest impact will happen if we position ourselves outwards as Kingdom-style leaders and ambassadors of heaven.

Discussion and Activation

How can you become better at discerning what the Holy Spirit is doing or saying?

To what extent do you see yourself as an ambassador for the Kingdom and how do you express this as you go about your daily life?

Which Kingdom-style leadership qualities do you exhibit and which would you like to develop?

Of the fruits of the Spirit listed in Galatians 5:22–23 – Love, Joy, Peace, Forbearance, Kindness, Goodness, Faithfulness, Gentleness and Self-control – which do you struggle with the most and what steps can you take to develop them?

9
Visionary, Hope-Filled Leader

Jesus exemplifies that Kingdom-style leadership is about being visionary and having a vision that centres on people. Visioning that focuses on anything other than people falls into the trap of becoming about ego and leads to exploitation. This is sadly what we witness in some organisations as they focus on the performance-for-profit model. As a 'sent' son or daughter there is a vision and purpose for you to live your life focused on relationships.

> Vision is the response that flows from the question
> 'How can I make the world better for others?'

When God created the earth and everything on it he was implementing a clear vision that made his work meaningful. If you think of all the leadership heroes throughout the Bible, be it Noah, Moses, David or Daniel in the Old Testament, or John the Baptist, Mary, Peter or Paul in the New Testament, they all had a vision that aimed for cultural transformation. In Jim Kouzes' and Barry Posner's book *Leadership Challenge*, they state that 'Being forward-thinking is the quality that most separates leaders from individual contributors.'[14]

Jesus came to earth with a very clear vision and this steered his ministry forward. The ability to receive visions creates vitality, focuses energy and clarifies purpose. On the flip side, when there is no vision, distraction, lethargy and desperation ensue. As Kingdom-style leaders we carry Jesus' vision: *'Therefore go and make disciples of all nations, baptising them in the name of the Father and of the Son and of the Holy Spirit'* (Matthew 28:19). God is keen to share with each of us our personal vision that further expands this calling. Mine is 'to change the face of leadership'. I encourage you to spend time with God, asking the question 'How do you want me to make the world better for others?' Allow him to fill your heart with his plans for you until your heart feels like it will burst if you do not respond.

Being able to receive visions feels like hope, and hope creates and energises that ability. Hope brings a feeling of expectation and desire for a particular thing to happen that may help or save an individual or group of people. Hope provides a foundation for believing that something good may happen and brings a feeling of trust. Society today often takes the word hope and uses it in a way that conveys uncertainty and doubt; for example, 'I hope it won't rain' or 'I hope so'. But the Bible teaches that hope flows from our faith in God and the confidence and security he provides, which removes all doubt from our minds. Romans 15:13 declares: *'May the God of hope fill you with all joy and peace as you trust in him, so that you may overflow with hope.'* Biblical hope is a confident expectation or assurance based upon God's truth and promises, which enables us to stand confidently and full of joy. To partner with any doubt and uncertainty is not God's intention. Hebrews 11:1 expresses such Kingdom Hope: *'Faith is confidence in what we hope for and assurance about what we do not see.'*

Several years ago I had a wonderful holiday abroad with a friend and our daughters which was only marred by problems we experienced with the villa swimming pool. It had drained and we were told it would take several days to fix and refill. Seeing the despondency on the girls' faces I prayed for God's blessing on our holiday, that in the morning the pool would be ready. Sure enough, when we got up the pool had miraculously filled, much to the delight of everyone and the complete surprise of the maintenance staff!

Our confidence comes with knowing for sure, without questioning, what we have been promised by God in his Word. Our faith is based on the confident assurance of our salvation through Jesus' victory on the cross. The phenomenal actions of the early Christians, recorded in Hebrews 11, were made possible because their faith was firmly rooted in their confidence and hope in God. You may be thinking that their situation was different to the difficult times we currently live in but, under Roman rule, their reality was one of persecution very much worse than what many, though not all, Christians encounter today. Not only were they severely persecuted they also lived through an era of sexual sin, immorality, idolatry and unhealthy living that was in stark contrast to the righteous lifestyle they chose to exemplify to those around. Despite these challenges, filled by the Holy Spirit, the early Christians turned the world upside down and Christianity rapidly grew. Let's not allow our circumstances to become an excuse, hiding from the world because we believe it is in freefall and hopeless. To challenge this perception, it is interesting to view Hans Rosling's 'The Joy of Stats' that illustrates how world poverty has decreased and our planet is a healthier place to live than it was 200 years ago.[15] Let's not reduce biblical hope to a misplaced feeling or hunch but instead recognise it as our reality and build our lives from this sure foundation – that God always keeps his promises. When you hear yourself say 'I hope so' check where this thought is coming from.

> It's not so much about lack of faith but a lack of hope

...so next time you are wondering why things are feeling a little hopeless, check your Kingdom Hope level.

Receiving visions partners with a foundation of hope. In contrast, Proverbs 13:12 warns that *'Hope deferred makes the heart sick, but a longing fulfilled is a tree of life.'* Without the cycle of both vision and hope, life can begin to feel rather futile, like a boat endlessly going round in circles because it does not know which port to steer towards. A leader without vision and hope becomes lost, along with those who decide to follow.

A visionary, hope-filled leader is consumed with making tomorrow better than today and settles for nothing less. They have the ability to be optimistic about the future whilst never being satisfied with the present, balancing being content and happy where they are with refusing to stay there. Visionary, hope-filled leaders refuse to be pessimistic and gloomy because they understand that,

> today's challenges are one step closer to tomorrow's solution and vision

Discontent breeds hopelessness which, when left unchecked, can turn into resignation. Resignation says I have given up, conceded defeat and what is undesirable is inevitable. It indicates the end of something and the question is, what are you saying has finished? The end of a dream, I'll never be able to make a difference, this person or place is beyond help, things are never going to change? When we live from a place of discontentment this list is endless. But what does our discontentment say to God? Discontentment reveals a lifestyle that lacks a godly fear and reverence because his Word declares that not only is he the overseer of all but also that he has a plan at all times. Whether we succumb to discontentment and hopelessness or not, the truth is that God is still on Plan A for the world. When we watch the international news and see the fallen-ness of man, God still has his plan. When things kick off in the office and we see unrest, God will turn chaos back to order as part of his plan. When we become discontent and hopeless, deviating away from God, he is still sticking to his plan. Despite our defiance and grumpy, rebellious-teenage behaviour, he continues to love and shepherd his children.

> Let's not allow the circumstances around us to dictate our stance on life.

Learn to stand in a place of thanksgiving and praise for the good we see that God has already provided, rather than focus on things that have not yet happened. Let's continue to praise our Father in heaven in reverence of him, shouting, 'No matter what, I trust you God.' This declares hope and contentment into the world for followers around us to embrace. God owes us no explanation for the difficult seasons and situations in our lives but he does promise to turn all things to good. Step by step, visionary, hope-filled leaders make the world a better place for others because they exude contentment, regardless of life's storms, becoming the beacons of light and hope that followers can't help but gravitate towards.

We easily fall into the trap of seeing work as something to tolerate and/or complain about, losing sight of the vision God has for us. Fuelled by our prayers and understanding of biblical truth, if there is one way in which we, as the body of Christ, should stand head and shoulders above others around us, it is our joy and hope-filled vision for tomorrow, not our grumbling and complaining of the status quo today.

Spend time with God, repent of wrong thinking from partnering with discontentment and hopelessness and, with the help of the Holy Spirit, turn your thinking towards his truth and an eternal perspective. Build firm prayer foundations, remembering who God is and who you are in him. Position yourself in prayer from the place of Jesus' victory on the cross and remind yourself daily of his goodness, his sovereignty over the world, his compassion and love. Remember that your prayers are powerful enough to turn around difficult situations and change the world. As you co-labour with God, learn to call out tomorrow's possibilities whilst being in the tension and confusion of today – be the light in dark places. Living from our identity as beloved sons and daughters gives us a sense of peace that we can lean on as the day unfolds. As a Kingdom-style leader,

> carry your vision and hope in your pockets and scatter
> all that God and his Kingdom have to offer

...as you go about your daily 'works'.

Discussion and Activation

What is the vision that God has placed in your heart to make tomorrow a better place?

How are you doing on your hope barometer and is it based on biblical truth or earthbound constraints?

Take time to read through the Gospels and record examples of Jesus' Kingdom-style leadership to his family and friends, disciples and all those around him. What are the qualities demonstrated?

10
Relational Leader 1: Born to be Relational

When coaching senior leaders I often challenge them around the statement that leadership is relational – it's about conversations and connection with people. Organisations can have the best vision statement, business plan, processes, systems and technology but without people these are voided. It's the people that breathe life in to any organisation. To be a good leader you have to be relational, to bring the best out of people and enable them to flourish, whether in your church, local community, school, office, hospital, factory, government building or home.

Jesus was an incredible, hope-filled visionary who also understood the importance of being relational. He exemplifies how to balance different types of relationships as he lived life with those around him sharing the gospel as he encountered various groups of people. He prioritised relationships in three ways: upwards, inwards and outwards.[16] Jesus spent significant time *upwards* in prayer with his Father, both intimate quiet time (just the two of them) and being 'connected' during his missional activities throughout the day. He understood that he could do nothing without his Father's help and would seek his continuous guidance. He prioritised time *inwards* with friends and the disciples, sharing life as he invested in them on a daily basis. Jesus modelled the new covenant principle not to travel alone, recognising the advantages of undertaking mission work with the love and support of others, though there were times when the disciples surely tested this resolve, as many leaders discover! Jesus gave himself *outwards* to the people who came to hear him teach and with whom he socialised beyond his inner circle of friends. Without 'going out', mission becomes insular and self-serving, selfishly keeping all God has to offer to ourselves.

In the same way, we need to learn how to be relational by balancing our up, in and out relationships: prioritising time with God, time with close friends and those we disciple, as well as being aware of how what we project outwardly impacts on others. This is easier said than done because being relational requires us to manage our feelings and emotions so that relationships remain authentic, healthy and strong, rather than becoming distant, painful and dysfunctional.

We are emotional beings and our emotions can steer us in many directions if we do not understand and effectively manage them. Good leaders recognise it is not just what they do but how they do it that makes the difference. How many times have you witnessed someone achieve a task or goal but fail to drive their emotions in the right direction, which has greatly reduced the effectiveness of the end result? Our mood and tone affect our message so to understand our emotions and how they drive behaviour is critical. Self-awareness, self-management and our ability to empathise through being socially aware, all have to be understood before we can positively manage our relationships in the way that Jesus demonstrated to us.

My 'Stuff', Your 'Stuff'

Good leaders find effective ways to understand and improve the way they handle their own and other people's emotions. I call this,

'managing my stuff' so that I can read and respond empathetically to your 'stuff!'

You can spot an emotionally mature leader by their ability not just to achieve tangibles such as getting results, but also in the all-important intangibles, for example higher morale, motivation and commitment. Leaders with a supportive emotional attitude who show empathy and bring the best out in people, have learnt something known as 'resonance'. They are excellent at finding common ground and building rapport. A family, team, church or organisation's ability to flourish or dissipate will depend to a large extent on the leader's effectiveness in managing their emotional intelligence.

When God created man he created an emotional being, illustrated by the array of emotions that Adam and Eve expressed in the Garden of Eden – a mixture of God's good and, sadly, Satan's negativity. We read in the New Testament that Jesus expressed an array of different emotions during his time on earth. The shortest verse found in the Bible is John 11:35, when Jesus was moved by compassion for Mary over the death of her brother Lazarus (before he raised him from the dead); it simply states, *'Jesus wept.'* Such an illustration teaches us that,

> emotions are very much a part of us and are neither right nor wrong

...it's our responses and actions that are important. Many are taught from childhood that emotions are bad, so we invest considerable time trying to ignore them, in the hope that they will just go away. They don't! They simply hang around like annoying back-seat drivers, blocking our ability to connect with our own feelings and build good relationships with others. We can easily learn to live by the emotional atmosphere of those around us, displaying inappropriate responses that go unchecked and give others a false impression of who we are. Many families do not encourage the expression of feelings and shut them down, preventing family members from being able to express how they truly feel. I once heard someone say that emotions are 'like wild plants that need to be cultivated, rather than poisonous plants that need to be eradicated'. So how are you doing at cultivating healthy responses to your own emotions?

Anger, Hostility and Conflict

As a child I was taught that anger was bad and must never be expressed. Unfortunately this led to many years of anger being suppressed inwardly that had a habit of negatively seeping out, impacting on my behavioural responses at home, school and then in the workplace. Anger is a powerful emotion that tells us that something is wrong, that we need to act in some way. This is illustrated in Matthew 21:12–13 when Jesus entered the temple courts and drove out all who were buying and selling there, declaring: *'It is written . . . "My house will be called a house of prayer," but you are making it "a den of robbers".'* Jesus was expressing his righteous anger because his Father's house was coming under disrepute. Anger is neutral, but its power can be used for constructive or destructive purposes.

Sadly, poorly expressed anger is what we witness around us, whether within families, between friends, in our workplace or more broadly at a national or international level. It is easy to confuse anger and hostility but they are different because,

> anger is an emotion, whereas hostility is an attitude.

Hostile people have developed a negative attitude to persons or events and when such hostility is left unchecked it hardens over time and becomes hatred. Both hatred and hostility are not God's design for us but belong to Satan's realm and are evil.

To reiterate: anger is not evil, it's neutral. It's how we deal with our anger that makes the difference in moments of conflict and to our own well-being. Put simply, 'conflict' happens when one person's concerns appear to be incompatible with those of others. A concern can be anything, a difference in opinion, idea, perspective, decision-making and prioritising approach, belief, ideology or a responsibility for another. Conflict escalates in stages: something happens and A blames B, which makes B react to A. Rather than seeking resolution at that stage, we often look for someone who will agree with us. This leads to antagonism and alliance-building as the two camps invest into the conflict. Sadly, when unchecked, this can escalate to open warfare, producing only winners and losers and, at worst, devastating destruction. Through these stages, the emotion of anger has shifted into an attitude of hostility and hate. Jesus encourages us to go to the person and, in private, talk through the issue openly and authentically with the aim of reconciliation.

How different the world would be if we, as person A or B, were emotionally mature enough to go immediately to the other person and seek reconciliation rather than fall into the trap of gossip, slander and seeking allies to support us which then escalates into open warfare. Interestingly, we are taught that conflict is bad but,

> managed conflict can act as a valuable catalyst

....enabling energy, challenging the status quo and so enabling a different way of being and working to flourish. A place devoid of conflict may lack innovation, creativity and inclusiveness that we associate with God's realm. Managed conflict results in greater engagement, trust and respect because people feel they have been listened to and understood. It leads to a better understanding of others and improved relationships because there is a new confidence that an issue will get resolved, which engenders greater productivity and better performance. So the challenge is finding the response that supports constructive rather than destructive responses by maturely handling our emotional responses. The tongue is one of the most powerful and lethal weapons in society. Used well it encourages, builds and edifies another individual but used poorly can harm and destroy. We reap what we sow, which is why 2 Corinthians 10:5 instructs us to *'take captive every thought to make it obedient to Christ'*.

Emotional maturity is underpinned by being aware of our thoughts and emotions, so we need to understand how our emotional responses work on a daily basis. Emotional intelligence is all about managing the self between an event and a response. When something happens a sensation enters the back of the brain near the spinal cord. Our primary senses enter here and have to travel to the very front of our brain before we can think rationally about our experience. To get there these sensations pass through the limbic system, the place where emotions are experienced. Emotional intelligence is about the ability to travel this pathway effectively from the back to the front of the brain. Billions of microscopic neurons line the road between the rational and emotional centres, with information travelling between them much like cars up and down a city street. Our emotional intelligence is greatly affected by our ability to keep this road well-travelled. The more we think about what we are feeling, and do something productive with that feeling, the more developed this pathway becomes. Because we spend considerable time ignoring our feelings or getting swamped by them, most lapses in emotional intelligence come from this simple lack of understanding and maturity.

Did you know you can experience an average of 27 emotions every hour? If you are awake for 16 hours that's around 430 emotional experiences from the time you get up until the time you go to bed; 3,000 that guide you through every week and more than 150,000 each year. This helps us understand why people who manage emotions effectively are easier to be with and more likely to achieve their objectives. Our emotions are on display 24 hours a day whether we are aware of this or not because 93 per cent of communication between people is non-verbal. We pick up the moods of our colleagues, family and friends even when they say nothing. The overflow of emotions and out-of-control emotional reaction is at the root of many conflicts and upsets.

> By changing the inner attitudes of our mind,
> we can shift the outer aspects of our lives

...and healthy relationships flourish. Our ability to influence directly, relates to our ability to be effective relationally and to do that we need to develop emotional maturity.

Jesus describes Satan as the 'father of lies' (John 8:44) and much of our stress, anxiety and negative responses to situations flow from believing those lies. The chatterbox voice in our thinking transmits negative thoughts about self and the people around us, and these lies impact on our expectations, govern our behaviour and lead us to view experiences in a way that re-enforces those lies. They become a repetitive loop playing with our thinking and when left unchecked become constraints, choking the abundant life God intended for us.

In James 1:6–8 he writes that a doubting person is *like a wave of the sea, blown and tossed by the wind. That person should not expect to receive anything from the Lord. Such a person is double-minded and unstable in all they do*. 'Unstable' comes from a Greek word meaning 'unsteady, wavering, in both his character and feelings'. A double-minded person is restless and confused in their thoughts, actions and behaviour, and they feel in conflict with themselves. Such inner conflict can prevent us from being able to lean confidently on God and his promises. We become like a drunken person, unable to walk straight, who sways with no defined direction and, as a result, doesn't get anywhere or, at worst, falls over. Such unsteady, double-mindedness can feel like a battleground in our mind, with the annoying back-seat chatterbox driver and our 'self-talk' voice transmitting all sorts of negative, ungodly comments that fuel an array of inappropriate emotional responses. This chatterbox voice is Satan's way of lying to us about our identity and it minimises our ability to impact positively on the world around us. His plan is to get into our heads and activate unhealthy thoughts and emotions to distract us.

The good news is that we have Christ in us, who combats any scheme that Satan tries to play in our minds; we just need to be aware of the battle strategy of both realms and side with the good team that has already won. Any time you revisit your past without remembering how God sees and loves you, you subject yourself to the spirit of deception, which is why we must guard against having any 'self-talk' that differs from God's truth. When we learn to deal with these tensions and work on our emotional intelligence we increase our ability to influence through developing and maintaining healthy relationships with family and friends and our place of work.

Discussion and Activation

How good are you at managing your up, in and out relationships?

As a child what were you taught about emotions and how to handle 'conflict'?

How good are you at managing the gap between when something happens and how you respond?

Do you control your thoughts and emotions or do they control you? What impact does this have on your ability to influence?

11

Relational Leader 2: Understanding Your Emotional Intelligence

To begin to understand how the pesky back-seat chatterbox driver has taken up residence in our thinking, controlling our emotional responses, let's explore how our belief system is created.

The Creation of Our Belief System

When we are born we come in to the world with a clean belief system, a bit like an empty computer disc. From day one we act like a sponge, gathering and absorbing information. Everything that happens to us – what we hear, see, smell, sense, feel and what we are told – is stored. We take things personally and at a very early age start to make positive and negative decisions about ourselves and the world around us.

Please hear my heart: parenting is the most challenging role anyone will ever undertake and, with the best will in the world, however hard we try, there will be times when we mess up. The purpose of this chapter is not to dishonour parents, because we are clearly commanded to respect them, but simply to recognise the impact they and others who influence us in our formative years have on the way our belief system is put together. Even with good parenting, what we absorb is based on our perception of events. Identical twins raised together in their early years, experiencing the same situations, will take in different information and their belief systems will be unique. We can desire to be good parents but

> there is only one perfect parent and his name is Father God,
> so give yourself a break, you can only do your best!

By the age of two we become more mobile and individually want to explore our world. We get positive feedback but also disapproval, often hearing the word 'No' 50,000 times by the age of five. Parents say 'No' to teach good values and behaviour as well as keeping a child safe, but often it is the energy of the 'No' that brings an interpretation or meaning that's stored into the belief system.

By seven we have sorted and neatly re-filed all the evidence, putting labels on the drawers and pigeonholes that describe how we see ourselves. From this place we start the comparison game, becoming more self-conscious and aware of how we match against other children, judging and comparing: 'Do I run faster?', 'Is she prettier?', 'Am I better at maths?', 'Is he more popular?', etc. At puberty our self-esteem and self-confidence become hormonally affected, increasing and decreasing our responses to our stored evidence: 'Nobody loves me', 'I'm stupid, ugly', 'Life is unfair'. This is often why teenagers can behave badly but not be in control of, or know why, they feel the way they feel; they have no way of processing their inner thoughts that the chatterbox voice is transmitting alongside the emotion and turmoil caused by the hormones running through their bodies.

We keep adding evidence to prove we are right about our beliefs, building a wall around each one. The older we get the bigger the wall. By adulthood we have created our own designer lenses that we look through based on our tailor-made belief system and it is this unique belief system that controls our adult responses, if left unchecked. Our negative, unhealthy thoughts about ourselves and the world around us get activated and go on display for everyone around to pick up. Similarly, other people's belief systems activate and everyone's responses collide with each other. This is the 'mood music' in the room that we sense, feel, hear and see. Often such mood music is nothing to do with the issue at hand but rather each person's set-up and emotional hurts from the past that have been activated. Emotional maturity results in resonance and harmony, but immature responses sound and feel like an orchestra that is out of tune and not in time with each other, which is very uncomfortable to listen to and be a part of. At the same time those involved often have no real understanding of what is actually happening in the room.

I once worked with two senior managers from the same department who had not spoken appropriately to each other for 18 months, resulting in the department becoming rather dysfunctional. One manager spent a lot of time investing into the conflict by seeking allies whilst the other had completely shut down to everyone around. The outward impression was a failing department but the underlying root cause was about the difficult relationships they each had with their own dads that they had each transferred to the other. By working through this with them individually, we were able to resolve the tension within their relationship, which resulted in both of them apologising to their senior team and thankfully things began to improve.

Sadly, such discord can be experienced at work but also in our homes, social friendships and church environments.

Understanding Triggers (Thought + Emotion)
So what gets activated that can be so beautiful or strike up such

discord? I describe this as a *trigger* – a sensitive spot in our belief system. It's the label on each filing cabinet drawer created in our early years that we are so convinced it is true it heavily influences our behavioural responses. It pushes us to feel, react and perform in certain ways that we are not consciously in control of. When a trigger is activated it can help us to achieve and do our best, but it can also cause us to hold back, create stress and/or harm our relationships with others and our self. When a negative trigger is activated the pathway across the brain does not function at its most efficient and rational. As a result, the junk stored in the limbic system ambushes our response, resulting in inappropriate and dysfunctional behaviour. Our reactions can cause us more problems than we had to begin with. When we are able to recognise our triggers, we can shrink them to the point that they won't negatively impact our actions by replacing them with godly truths that we can firmly stand on.

My brother and I grew up with different things spoken over us from our parents. My brother regularly heard 'You are bright but just need to try harder!' I heard, 'Well done, Karen, you always try so hard!' Listening to both, the negative belief that 'I'm not clever so to succeed I must work hard' became rooted in my thinking. I began to live by my school report summary: 'Karen is a sensible little girl who always tries her best.' 'Work hard to get the job done' was my expectation for myself and those around me, which developed into overbearing and controlling leadership. By recognising the lies I believed about myself and creating a positive expectation rooted in 'Lighten up, I can do this' I am much more fun to work alongside (though I still have my moments!). I no longer feel I have to work hard to keep up or prove myself. Of course, being secure in my identity I know I don't have to perform to be loved by Father God. I am free to be me, working from approval not for approval.

So, what exactly are these triggers that have such an effect on people's lives?

> A trigger consists of a thought plus an emotion.

The thought can be positive or negative and the emotion can be any one of an array of feelings we experience each day. The amount of emotion attached to the thought determines the size and potential impact of the trigger. The key emotions released are: JOY (including happiness, love and feeling excited), ANGER (including frustration, irritation and boredom i.e. how dare the world not stimulate me!), SADNESS (and feeling miserable), GUILT, SHAME and FEAR. Guilt and shame often get confused but guilt is around 'what I've done' whereas shame is 'who I am', e.g. I am a nuisance to everyone, I am useless, I am worthless. Below is a list of triggers that may help you identify those you have stored. When people first look at this list, usually six to eight words will resonate and these are the ones to start with. Allow God to highlight those triggers that have become rooted in your belief system. Start to become aware of these as you go about your daily life and note how often they get activated. Be aware when you speak them over yourself, for example 'I'm so stupid' or 'No one cares'. Don't worry if you are initially unable to change your response as the first step is just to recognise the trigger moment. Triggers can work like dominoes; once one is pushed others follow suit. The triggers I watch out for are related to 'Responsible', 'Be Perfect', 'Be Strong' and when they activate together they can make my behaviour dysfunctional if I am not managing 'my stuff'.

A selection of triggers

Alone	Impatient	Responsible
Abandoned	Intolerant	Stupid
Authority	Injustice	Trust
Bad	Invisible	Ugly
Be Perfect	Irresponsible	Undeserving
Be Strong	Less Than	Unimportant
Better Than	Loss	Unlovable
Betrayed	Loyalty	Unsafe
Commitment	Manners	Unsupported
Controlled	Money	Unwanted
Controlling	Not Good Enough	Unworthy
Critical	Out of Control	Valueless
Disregarded	Powerless	Victim
Disrespected	Public Embarrassment	Weak
Duty	Rebel	Worry
Equality	Rejection	Wrong
Failure	Respect	

Start to recognise your regular triggers as you become more aware of their patterns in your life and this will help define whether they are small, medium or large.

Triggers are more likely to activate if you are feeling tired, stressed, unwell and generally out of balance. If you have spent many years perfecting how to keep out of touch with your emotions, it can be difficult to identify these events. The following list may help you to identify triggers based on your learnt behavioural responses. By identifying the behaviour, you can link which triggers are activated e.g. comparing yourself to others may link to 'Not Good Enough' (NGE), 'Unworthy' or 'Be Perfect':

Triggers based on learnt emotional responses

- Feeling better than others: my car is bigger, my job is better, etc.
- Judging yourself and others
- Comparing yourself to others
- Saying 'I should' often
- Saying 'I can't' regularly
- Sacrificing too much (over allow, can't say 'no')
- Feeling lesser than others
- Fear of change
- Fear of making mistakes
- Big fish in a small pond; stay in comfort zone
- Lying/not telling the truth
- Breaking agreements often
- Spending time with people who feel/act/talk negatively
- Your friends complain a lot
- Feeling/acting/talking negatively or as a victim
- Can't say how you really feel
- Rejecting people who love you
- Inability to give to yourself
- Inability to participate fully
- Watch a lot of TV
- Not taking holidays
- Poor personal hygiene.

The hardest part to understanding our behavioural responses is identifying the triggers and recognising that, as you project them into the world, they are reflected back on you. It's a vicious cycle of,

'the more I believe IT the more I see IT, and the more I see IT, the more I believe IT'.

As events occur we dip in and out of our belief system to see where we have experienced this before and seek to prove it's right, over and over. This is the deception Satan has used over the years to slowly trap you. If you have an NGE trigger you'll look for evidence to prove you are not good enough. You see everything in the world that reinforces that you are not good enough and only see the world through your NGE lens. Such triggers not only distort your vision and responses, they shout so loud it becomes hard to hear God's voice. Unconsciously, you flash your signals into society and the person or people who are most attracted to that signal will appear. The good news is that once you have identified your triggers you can stop bonding with them and replace them with a positive truth. This effectively disarms them so that they no longer have such a negative impact. Begin to,

choose to see yourself as God sees you and stop buying into Satan's deception.

Satan is not creative so there will be two or three lies that continuously come up that key in to all your triggers, usually around fear of failure and fear of rejection. Particularly be on your guard to recognise that the breakthrough is often preceded by a barrage of deceit by Satan. Learn to recognise Satan's inadequate game plan and practise 'request denied' to his lies. Do not let him move you away from being focused on Jesus because what you allow yourself to tolerate will dominate your thinking and actions. The bigger the vision, the more Satan will try and attack. Focus on the Kingdom of Heaven and turn his accusation into intercession: 'You're right, on my own I can't but with God I can!' Bring the lie into the light, make a decision to no longer accede to the lie and replace it with the truth. Ask God, 'Is there a lie I believe about you?' As he shares this with you, follow the process of repenting and renouncing the lie. Give the lie to God and ask him to replace it with the truth. God is kind, he always responds.

The Impact of 'Golden Rules' in Childhood

As well as identifying triggers you need to understand the impact of the 'golden rules' that were said to you as a child growing up because these rules and your triggers interconnect. Triggers go off when a 'rule' becomes challenged, because either you or others around you do not attain the right standard. Once you recognise the negative impact of such triggers, you can choose to respond differently by rewriting them. The following list gives examples that may help you to identify your 'golden rules', though it is not exhaustive:

- Be respectful (no answering back/rudeness)
- 'I want' never gets (ask nicely)
- Speak only when spoken to (don't interrupt)
- Mind your manners: say please and thank you
- Keep everything clean and tidy
- Always tell the truth
- If you make a promise, always keep it
- Be loyal to those around you
- Be on time and don't keep others waiting
- Leave the table only when everyone's finished
- Finish what you started/what's on your plate
- Work hard to gain respect/earn your status/prove yourself
- There's no such thing as can't
- If you want something doing right, do it yourself
- Failure is not an option (shows weakness)
- Stick up for yourself and don't let people walk all over you
- Be careful who you trust (trust no one).

Write down the top 'golden rules' that you regularly had to listen to as you grew up. Then consider out of a score of 1 to 10 how strong they are (10 being the highest) and how the rule translates into the way you communicate and lead others.

Start to recognise when they are negatively impacting on your responses and make a choice to respond differently.

I had a client who looked at the list and immediately identified with the golden rule about 'leaving the table only when you have finished everything on your plate'. When we explored how this was impacting on his leadership he suddenly looked sheepish, exclaiming that he needed to apologise to someone because he had been unfair. His translation of 'finishing everything on your plate' was 'you can't go home until all your work is finished'! A member of his team had left on a previous Friday without completing something he was working on that did not need to be finished that day, but my client had reacted inappropriately on the following Monday morning.

I was raised with a 9-scoring trigger underpinned by 'treat others as you would want to be treated'. This is a positive belief but when people do not meet my 9/10 expectation I can go into negative reaction. Similarly I had another golden rule, 'If you start something always finish it properly', which is the foundation of my 'Be Perfect' and 'Responsibility' triggers. This rule can lead me into a neurotic perfectionist expectation over myself and others if I don't catch it. There is no quick-fix model to understanding your emotional intelligence but by giving time to identifying both triggers and your entrenched 'golden rule' beliefs you can learn how to start the process of disarming their negative impact, which in turn draws people closer to you. As we become more able to understand the truth of who we are and walk with godly values and beliefs we are better positioned to become effective relational influencers.

Discussion and Activation

What triggers have you identified? Which tend to activate together? How do your triggers impact on your life?

What childhood 'golden rules' have you identified and how do they impact your communications and ability to lead others around you?

What impact do your triggers and the chatterbox voice have over your willingness to step out through covert and overt operations?

12
Relational Leader 3: Maturing Your Emotional Intelligence

Leadership matters to God and to each and every one of us, both as a leader and follower. As leaders we must learn how to look after our physical, emotional and spiritual health because in moments of leadership you affect the well-being of those people around you. Be intentional in developing your emotional intelligence by letting go of unhealthy beliefs and move towards new, positive beliefs that bring freedom. As you identify your triggers and childhood 'golden rules' and so recognise their effect on your life, you can start to disarm their negative impact. This is all about redefining the gap, changing what you do with the moments between a challenging stimulus and how you choose to respond.

The Belief Tree

In Matthew 7:18 we read that *'A good tree cannot bear bad fruit, and a bad tree cannot bear good fruit. Every tree that does not bear good fruit is cut down and thrown into the fire.'* This is why we must ensure our thought processes align with God's opinion of us. By changing the inner attitudes of your mind your outer behaviour shifts and you become able to influence far more effectively. Imagine yourself as a tree. All that is above ground level reflects your outward behaviour that is seen by others and yourself. The roots of the tree are your inner beliefs, judgements and vows said to you, or you said over yourself, that feed your tree's behaviour. To change your negative behaviour you must understand what lies at the root, cut it off and replace with a positive one so that a positive 'fruit' can flourish. Our deeply rooted vows are a defence mechanism we employ as a response to negative words, experiences or situations to protect ourselves from being hurt. They go something like, 'I'll never . . .'. Deep-rooted judgements are critical, condemning judgements of others and reflect a refusal or an inability to forgive e.g. 'trust no one' or 'authority does not fix things'. Inner beliefs often flow from the 'golden rules' e.g. 'Failure is not an option', 'Speak only when spoken to'.

Have a go at drawing your own tree of behaviours, identifying your inner beliefs, deep-rooted vows and judgements that feed your behaviour. The example at the end of this chapter may help. Much of the information will flow from your triggers and 'golden rules'. Pray into this and ask God what he wants to highlight to bring you to greater freedom. Talk this through with trusted friends who will both encourage and challenge you to liberate yourself from your negative 'fruit tree' and construct a positive one. You may also find it beneficial to seek professional counselling support in order to process the past and its impact on you so that you are able to walk in freedom.

Achieving a Healthy Balance in Life

Triggers are most likely to go off when you are tired, stressed and out of balance. The following actions are about building balance into your life to ensure your triggers are minimised and kept in check:

- Prioritise your time with God. We don't have to be having a good day before we go to him. He is there for us however our day is panning out and loves to be part of everyday life. We feel so much better when we allow him in, sharing the joys and disappointments and hearing his affirmation over us, both at home and in our workplace. He has a creative solution to every situation and is great fun to be with.

- Go to God to express emotions and allow him to re-balance you. When you are facing a challenging situation, ask God, 'What can I do to bring more balance to myself and this situation?' Then ask, 'How can I choose to move forward, in the light of what I have learned?' This simple two-step process will help you to 'deal with your trigger and let it go'.

- Reward your mistakes. Learn from the situation and let go rather than beat yourself up. This includes being quick to ask for forgiveness and forgiving others. Treat yourself because of what you have learnt and choose to move forward.

- Don't put on the landing lights for negative thoughts and beliefs about yourself and others because this inevitably enables them to land. Recognise they are lies and say 'request denied'. Replace with positive truths such as 'I do belong here' or 'I am wonderfully made'. Deal with stuff as and when it comes up by breaking agreement with unhealthy beliefs and emotional hurts.

- Learn to be honest and authentic with your thoughts and feelings when communicating with those around you rather than wearing a mask. Masks push people away whereas being real with people enables them to come closer.

- List and celebrate successes and share these with God, family and friends; congratulate yourself alongside thanking God.

- List and celebrate what you are grateful for every day, including experiences that bring fulfilment. This helps to cultivate a heart of gratitude that God is good, even when we face difficult times.

- When people acknowledge you, absorb it and say 'thank you'. Accept acknowledgements, not just in your head but deep in your heart, because deep down you know you are worth it, because God says so.
- Don't waste time and energy comparing yourself to others. Comparison is futile because you are unique and have your own race to run that God has set out before you. No one else can run your race and you can't run theirs, so stop trying to do this. If you keep looking at others running around you, you'll run slower or, at worst, trip yourself up! Enjoy running your race.
- Be aware of how you handle others' successes or failures and learn to honour them with humility and grace.
- When you have an issue with an individual, deal with 'your stuff', then go to that person, share how you feel and work together to resolve the situation with the aim of reconciliation (Matthew 18:16). Not everyone thinks the same as you so be intentional around displaying love to those who think and feel differently.
- Practise forgiveness. By recognising your triggers choose a path of forgiveness rather than sitting in judgement on others or yourself. Forgiveness is an act of will from which freedom flows and we must not base decisions on how we feel, but on truth. Holding a grudge keeps you captive so leave the judging to God. You may be unclear as to why God allowed something awful to happen but he always provides a way out through the freedom that Jesus secured on the cross. Process 'your stuff' and forgive others for theirs (whatever it is), remembering that forgiving someone does not say 'what you did was OK', rather 'I am choosing to let go'. Forgiveness is not something we do for other people but for ourselves. It prevents us from becoming hard of heart and enables us to

stay healthy both emotionally and spiritually; in this way we are able to move forwards.

- Learn when to say 'no' rather than over-allowing to others. When we are over-accommodating we place ourselves on a wheel, rather like a hamster going around, that creates resentment and disappointment because our needs are not met. We react negatively and then, out of our guilt, set ourselves up to sacrifice again (often referred to as 'over compensating'). Become good at expressing your needs when communicating with others, whether at work, family and friends or church, to help prevent going on the wheel of seemingly inexplicable reaction in the first place.

- Have a 'should' free day. Instead of having a superhuman list, prioritise what is important for today; the rest can simply wait.

- When you lose sight of who you are, the temptation is to seek affirmation elsewhere. Learn to treat yourself with honour and respect. By doing this you will project honour outwards and enable honour to be reflected back.

- Participate in life: a job that you love, friends, family, activities that you enjoy. Balance time with your partner, family and friends and 'me time'. Treat yourself by participating in the things *you* enjoy.

- Plan rest time each week. Your body is not designed to work 24/7. Use rest for quality time with God, family and friends but also time for yourself.

- Look after your body. Be aware of what you eat and drink and your sleep and exercise patterns. Go to the doctor and dentist regularly. Your body is the temple for the Holy Spirit so make it a pleasant place for him to inhabit.

- Plan and take your full holiday entitlement at regular intervals throughout the year and use this time to refresh –

this includes stay-at-home mums. When my children were younger I would purposely build in 'just me days' at the end of school holidays so that I could recharge my batteries doing things I enjoyed. On holiday means no laptop or work mobile because the world of work can carry on without you.

- Set and write down goals and dream big with God and review these regularly. We have a generous Father in heaven who loves to lavish his children and it is great fun seeing dreams fulfilled.
- Define clear boundaries for what in your life is negotiable and what is not, e.g. working hours, what to commit your time to, which areas to serve at church, etc., and stick to them. This will help you keep focused on your goals.

You may find the following physical techniques help you to let go of triggers:

- Take 10 deep breaths.
- Do some imaginary drumming, boxing bag or dancing. Use physical exercise to help shift your emotional state.
- Laughter is a great tonic, particularly laughing at the lies of Satan as you replace them with truth. Have some good films or comedians handy that make you laugh. Allow sadness and tears when this is how you feel – big boys can cry! Again, use films or music to help you release sadness.

Living from a Place of Freedom

In Exodus 3:1–3 we read that God called out to Moses from the burning bush and commissioned him to lead the Israelites, God's people, out of Egypt to freedom. From a place of self-doubt and emotional immaturity Moses used a number of excuses as he tried to discount himself from the vision that God had for his life: 'You've got the wrong person', 'I'm not ready yet', 'What if I fail', 'I don't have the skills and there must be someone else better qualified' – these were Moses' stalling tactics but God was having none of it. Yet from such a hesitant start Moses went on to be one of the greatest leaders in the Bible. First and foremost he learnt that in God's presence there is fullness and apart from God he could do nothing. When Moses led the Israelites across the Red Sea they moved from slavery to freedom, and in the same way Jesus has offered us freedom to be who we have been created to be. We no longer have to remain captive to limiting beliefs that hold us back and prevent us walking in our full calling and destiny as children of God and ambassadors of the Kingdom. Don't allow yourself to make excuses, as Moses initially did, and stop discounting yourself by allowing your emotional intelligence to hold you captive; instead, make a decision to move forwards.

> Whether it is fear, habit or misunderstanding,
> seek to identify what is holding you back

...so that you can shift negative thinking to one that reflects who you truly are. If you allow the battle in your mind to take over, you will struggle to realise your vision and purpose. If negativity ensues this can breed disunity, which is just what Satan wants. Disunity leads us to read people and situations incorrectly based on wrong beliefs and we find ourselves blown off course.

I find it sad how the Israelites experienced one of the most incredible supernatural signs and wonders ever seen by man when God parted the Red Sea, but within two years lost sight of the goal that God had promised them. Despite God being there with them, miraculously providing food and water, they saw the walk to the treasure ahead of them as impossible and started to complain and grumble rather than having hearts full of gratitude. They forgot they were freed men and women and slipped back into self-inflicted slavery because they lost the battle in their minds. Don't make the same mistake by losing sight of who God has created you to be and what he has designed for you. Instead keep auditing yourself at the door around 'my stuff, your stuff'; be aware of any lies and unhealthy beliefs you are buying into and keep declaring the truth.

> Don't travel alone on this journey; travel with trusted friends

...you can be honest with and with whom you can express how you truly feel, who will love you and keep you accountable. Learn to be an emotionally mature, relational leader in order to bring the influence of the Kingdom to those around you.

Belief Tree Example

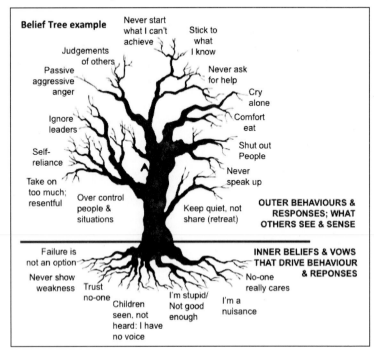

Discussion and Activation

From the 'Achieving a healthy balance in life' list, which particularly resonate for you that would be good to work on?

Have a go at creating your belief tree. Remember the goal is to shift your negative inner beliefs and judgements (the roots of your belief tree) to positive ones so that your responses and behaviours bear fruit. Review your tree at regular intervals as God reveals more lies in the future and you continue to mature emotionally.

13
Honouring Leader: Collaboration and a Serving Heart

Having witnessed many wonderful people promoted into leadership over the years, I am curious but also concerned to observe a pattern that befalls a number of them. They begin with all good intentions but then some sort of short circuit in the wiring of the brain brings about a change in their behaviour. A window gets opened and out flies their humility, compassion and integrity, in exchange for arrogance, pride and/or control, which affects the atmosphere around that leader making them difficult to work for. Such behaviour is often a cover-up for the inner emotion of fear as they battle in their mind various unhelpful lies that they should either know everything and have all the answers as the person 'in charge' or be seen as a fraud or not good enough. What can result is a newly appointed leader, consciously or subconsciously, isolating and positioning themselves in a hierarchy above those around them. Some develop an air of entitlement, behaving as if the perks of position are theirs by right. This type of ungodly characteristic can go on for years if not checked. The higher up the ladder of success they go, the worse their character and behaviour can become. They are not leading from the Kingdom awareness that those who exalt themselves will be humbled and those who humble themselves will be exalted. It's important we exalt God and allow him to root out any self-righteousness in our hearts. There is no room for pride, only humility and our cry must be 'more of you and less of me'.

Whatever we are feeling and whatever we are facing, God is always the answer. Any ungodly character and behaviour goes against the previously discussed qualities that followers seek in a leader, particularly those demonstrating personal integrity and practising what they preach. The principle that leadership is a privilege and you are there to serve your team and not the other way around gets lost or, in extreme cases, is never evident. This type of behaviour forces people to follow by compliance rather than commitment and leads to the disgruntlement aired with family and friends beyond the walls of 'work' where it feels safe to do so. At a personal level, many of us have to learn to navigate the follower, therefore 'less', pathway with leaders and 'colleagues' not just in our workplace but, sadly, sometimes in the church. Across all the areas of influence people will tolerate such poor leadership because they feel they have no choice, but their motivation, productivity and attendance are reduced. Others will simply vote with their feet and go elsewhere, seeking opportunities in a different department or organisation.

Whether in a formal leadership role or just through the opportunities you have to show Kingdom-style leadership, challenge yourself (and not just once) by asking, 'Am I guilty of misusing my position?', 'Am I serving my own ends to boost my ego or confidence rather than working for the good of those around me?'

If there is pride in your heart it will be expressed in one of three ways. Firstly, through *self-righteousness* that results from feeling insecure, the need to prove yourself or a 'better than' attitude. Secondly, through *self-reliance*, having to be strong, not trusting others or knowing how to build relationships. Thirdly, *self-pity*, focusing on the negatives with a lack of joy, feeling unappreciated and unloved. The 'pity party' discontent place is all about me, how life stinks, nobody cares.

> Whatever pride masquerades as, it does not belong in the weaponry of a Kingdom-style leader

...because it blocks our ability to serve others, whether we are a leader or a follower. Any trace of pride means you are simply connecting to the wrong realm and getting your worth from the wrong person.

Servant Leadership

If leadership is an opportunity to demonstrate an act of immense humble generosity, this requires the leader to position themselves with a serving heart towards others, with humility at the centre. Philippians 2:6–7 says of Jesus, *'Who, being in very nature God, did not consider equality with God something to be used to his own advantage; rather, he made himself nothing by taking the very nature of a servant, being made in human likeness.'*

On a daily basis, how we live, work, make decisions and serve the interests of those around us needs to flow from our first allegiance: to God himself. In doing so, we follow the example of Jesus who took on *'the very nature of a servant'*. We can reflect his approach in the way we handle a difficult colleague, encourage a challenging child or help a friend or stranger struggling with a situation. We do not do this to gain favour with God, because he is not in the performance management business, but from an assurance that we are already loved and have eternal life in Jesus. Servant leaders value the development of their followers, build their communities, act authentically and share power. In Matthew 20:25–26 we read: *'Jesus called them together and said, "You know that the rulers of the Gentiles lord it over them, and their high officials exercise authority over them. Not so with you. Instead, whoever wants to become great among you must be your servant.'* Servant Leaders who are secure in their identity and emotionally mature do not hold followers back because of their own insecurities or triggers that might threaten their significance. They have learnt to 'deal with it and let it go'. This enables them to let their followers run past as they cheer them on and they continue to celebrate their advances and successes. They do not allow their jealousy or competitiveness to hamper a follower in any way, including becoming a greater leader.

Culture of Honour

I mentioned earlier the teaching that I include in leadership development programmes around the culture of honour, which I believe sits at the heart of servant leadership.[17]

> The definition of 'to honour' is 'to respect or venerate; to hold in high esteem'.

Accordingly, a person who is honoured is so regarded. Under the Kingdom design of what I believe business in heaven will look like my desire is to encourage those I teach to collaborate with each other through developing a culture of honour. That they will choose at all times and at all levels to recognise and acknowledge worth and to act accordingly with each other through mutual respect, honesty and sincerity. Having set the seeds of these thoughts with leaders, I get them to consider what collaboration through a culture of honour looks and feels like at a personal, team and organisational level and, equally importantly, to their customers and clients. Equally to consider the effect of dishonour on that view. Encouraging others to work together collaboratively through the culture of honour focuses on summoning the best out of people and bringing them together to work in a spirit of unity and encouragement, to produce something they would be unable to do alone.

I was asked to facilitate a team development day for around thirty-five people. As the first part of the morning unfolded I was sad to witness that as each of the team leaders reported on the progress of their region, the response from colleagues in the room was not very respectful. They were either comparing results or not listening, which resulted in a 'golf clap' at the end of each mini presentation – the half-hearted clap people do because it is the thing to do rather than because they want to encourage the 'performer'. Something within me wanted to challenge this response. As soon as I was introduced I covertly took the opportunity to begin to teach Kingdom-style leadership around the culture of honour. I discussed with them how amazing it was to hear the results from each team and the hard work behind the statistics they'd shared. I mentioned that one team's victory is another team's victory and, in the same way, that if a team is struggling then it is an issue for everyone to offer support and help resolve the situation. I finished my introduction by asking all those in the room to partake in a hearty clap for everyone because they are all so amazing. Thankfully the group caught what I was saying and followed my lead, which was a relief as I would otherwise have looked pretty silly, though in my heart I knew it was right to challenge their behaviour. What was interesting was that, at the end of the day when we reviewed key learning, several groups highlighted what they had learnt around the culture of honour and how it had made them feel good and part of the wider team.

If we act with the servant heart of Jesus in our workplace environment, we cannot help but see those around us grow and flourish as they are touched by the love of Christ. When we take time to listen to a work colleague's problems, despite our own situation, we are valuing them above ourselves; when we help a stranger with an act of kindness, this demonstrates Jesus' love and says to them 'you are worth it'. In these situations we are working to Kingdom priorities rather than earth-based deadlines and get this incredible opportunity to honour people in God's eyes. Even when the other person does not reciprocate it is important to remain resilient and keep projecting honour.

> Having taught a group of outpatient leaders the culture of honour, one of the senior nurses caught up with me some weeks later and despondently shared how she had made an effort to honour a difficult patient but their response had been very dishonouring in return. 'What's the point!' she exclaimed. I explained that honour is not dependent on a positive response but rather our choice to honour regardless of how people react. It was wonderful to see the penny drop and gave her a new desire to keep expressing honour to each patient, even the more persistently challenging ones.

As we seek to lead as role models, guard against your behaviour having a negative impact.

> A senior manager arrived at one of his coaching sessions very animated and frustrated. As he ranted about his team's poor performance and their inability to respond to his demands as the boss, he suddenly stopped, looked at me and, as the penny dropped, accepted his part in the situation. He had not realised his style of working did not match the team's

planned and organised preferences, and that there was a need to adjust his last-minute approach to deadlines rather than cause panic and havoc amongst the team. Coaching him via covert operations allowed the client to see his impact and encouraged the manager to apologise to the team in order to restore relationships and move forwards. By introducing a healthier, honouring leadership approach, this made a real difference.

> Honouring leadership is about where do I position myself to bring the best out of the other person

...not what do I expect you to do for me. There is no place in leadership for greed and self-indulgence. I like the quote from Joyce Meyer: 'Grow to the point that one of your first thoughts each morning in your heart is about how you can bless someone else that day.'[18] Look for the best in people, the nugget of gold rather than the coal that is still forming. Jesus had three years to develop his disciples. He mentored and coached them as they went about their life together through a model of learn, apply, review (what is called reflector learning style in business). He released the disciples at the earliest opportunity through on-the-job training, baptising and praying with people as they travelled together and he recognised that there would be mishaps on the way.

> As a leader, become the best encourager you can

...bringing out not only the earthbound talents but also biblical encouragement of how God sees that person through heavenly revelation, even when they don't see it themselves. Many saw Peter as an uneducated fisherman and a bit of a clumsy, loose cannon but Jesus saw the hidden truth. He made him part of the inner circle of disciples so that he could prepare him for his future destiny, which came to fruition as recorded in the book of Acts. Also described in Acts is how Ananias and Barnabas, through servant leadership and their obedience to God, prophesied and encouraged the apostle Paul in the early years of his ministry, enabling him to see his destiny and encouraging him at a time when he was seen as a persecutor of Christians and somewhat risky to be associated with.

> I once had a senior manager sent for coaching after being put on a performance review following grievances lodged against him for inappropriate, aggressive behaviour. Undeterred by the head of HR's fear that he might act aggressively towards me I agreed to meet the gentleman, knowing God would protect me. As the client ranted at how unfairly he had been treated I asked God to show me his heartfelt path for the individual. This gave me the way in: to express my sadness at how misunderstood he felt. From the moment I did that, his mood music shifted, the wall was breached and God's love covertly poured in.

I love that prophecy and encouragement so often go hand in hand. It is important to encourage followers when they have done well but also to prophesy what has thus far been unseen that God is revealing.

> Enable each person to see what they can become

...in the same way that Jesus and Barnabas did. Sadly, some will not make it, for example Judas Iscariot, but we need to uphold our belief in each person, to nurture their potential and believe in them more than they believe in themselves.

Serve well those you are developing by giving time to them as you go through life together, whether in a church setting or your workplace. Building a sense of family and community is important in our place of work and it saddens me how little people know about colleagues or take the time to get to know each other because of the pressure of constant deadlines.

Working with a team, I felt God encourage me to do an icebreaker relating to 'the common factor', identifying things they had in common with each other. They were shocked and pleasantly surprised to realise not only did they all have a passion for travel but also all enjoyed various types of cookery. Having these two things in common helped to build greater team spirit. They subsequently created an atmosphere of mutual support and encouragement and shared the results of each other's culinary skills at work. Let's face it, food and hospitality are a great team-building approach, exemplified by Jesus. It's good to break bread together; it builds a sense of community.

People develop through being around the gift of leadership, not just attending a leadership training course. Encourage people to develop independently as you enable, release and empower them, and see their self-belief expand. The disciples constantly let Jesus down but he stuck with them even when stupidity got in the way. Do not dismiss people but deal with your own disappointment as they have to deal with how you have disappointed them! Help them through and stick with them. Allow followers to grow as leaders by encouraging them to be who they are in God and by taking responsibility – running the race together but each knowing their part in that race. The more you get to know your followers the easier it is to know when they are ready to fly. Deuteronomy 32:11 reads: *'like an eagle that stirs up its nest and hovers over its young, that spreads its wings to catch them and carries them on its pinions'*. This is such a powerful image of leadership, that a mother eagle nurtures and raises her youngsters but knows the time to push them out of the nest, hovering alongside and sweeping them up on her wings should they not quite make it. She puts them back in the nest and tomorrow they try again until all the eaglets are able to fly. The statement that leadership is an act of immense, humble generosity simply means to walk with grace, mercy and humility. People mess up, intentionally or unintentionally, no matter what their position or status. As a Kingdom-style leader recognise this and, rather than a punitive response, accept in these moments that if you allow grace and mercy to flow, the individual gets an opportunity to grow and move forwards. Grace is getting what you don't deserve and mercy is not getting what you deserve. Human forgiveness waits to see change and if it does not happen we stubbornly refuse to forgive but this is not God's desire for us. Jesus cleared our debts on the cross, so to not offer this hand of grace, mercy and forgiveness to others is to disrespect what he achieved at Calvary for you and me. Acting with conviction from a stance of love, grace and mercy says 'you made a mistake, now let's fix it together' whereas condemnation says 'you are a mistake and unfixable'. There is no honour in condemnation.

Part of your Kingdom armoury is the powerful combination of encouragement and honour. I try to take every opportunity I can to wield this in the hope that people around me absorb it.

Nearing the end of a team development programme I often invite the senior leaders to stand in a circle and, starting with the most senior leader, ask them to thank each other and share what they value about their colleagues, publicly demonstrating their appreciation. This is a profound experience that bonds a team at a completely different level, and my hope is that they then go back to the office and work at this together in their teams. In another exercise I call 'Sorry, Thank you, Please', I instruct the team members to say what they are sorry about and apologise, what they want to thank others for and to ask with a 'please' for help they need from colleagues. This activity helps to build both authenticity and honour amongst the members of the team and encourages hope for the future as they learn to operate differently together. I challenge people to spot the treasure and call it out unashamedly. I had feedback from one senior manager that the team development day had 'moved the team beyond their wildest dreams'. Honour and forgiveness are a powerful combination.

Nehemiah led by setting an example and serving the good of others; this is an example of a leader who had an honouring, servant heart. We read in Nehemiah 5:15–16, *'The earlier governors – those preceding me – placed a heavy burden on the people and took forty shekels of silver from them in addition to food and wine. Their assistants also lorded it over the people. But out of reverence for God I did not act like that. Instead, I devoted myself to the work on this wall.'* He saw the hardship the people had to endure and waived his rights as the city governor to take a tax that would have provided him with luxury away from the poverty of those around him. His heart wept for the broken-down walls and people of Jerusalem and he longed to see both rebuilt, devoting himself to both and fighting off any opposition that came their way. Nehemiah loved God and brought everything before him. He was both a visionary, hope-filled leader but also a man of good character who was prepared to take action by demonstrating his faith in his work. His life showed in practical ways his love for God, for his people, his commitment to the task at hand, and his passion for justice. As an honouring leader, Nehemiah was not only a role model; he also demonstrated that,

> God's work, done in God's way and time, will be fruitful

...which is a great encouragement as we step out into our area(s) of influence. You may feel the task God calls you to do is insignificant compared to that of Nehemiah but God does not measure in this way. Jesus spoke about the significance of giving just a cup of cold water to others (Matthew 10:42). Seemingly small acts of love and service done in Jesus' name may carry greater value in eternity than all our most treasured achievements.

In our daily lives there are many opportunities to express honour-based, servant leadership so let's take these opportunities whenever they arise. In God's Kingdom everyone is treated with honour, dignity and respect and that's what we desire to create *'on earth as it is in heaven'*.

Discussion and Activation

As a leader are you guilty of misusing your leadership position to serve your own ends and boost your ego? If yes, is this behaviour driven by fear of failure and/or fear of rejection, or something else?

How can you encourage collaboration through the culture of honour in your area(s) of influence? What might this look like at personal, team and organisational levels, and to your clients and customers?

Who are your followers and how are you developing them?

Do you fill your pockets with mercy and grace to hand out to others as you go about your day? How can you make this a part of your daily life?

14
Courageous Leader

Many Christians receive teaching on the subject of servant leadership: to be kind, compassionate, honest and trustworthy and serving people in a way that reflects Jesus' character. If we focus on just servant leadership we miss the opportunity to demonstrate the fullness of Jesus' leadership in the way that he brought his mighty power and presence *'on earth as it is in heaven'*. As sons and daughters,

> we get to honour and serve by courageously expressing all God's Kingdom, seeing people healed, restored and set free.

Stepping out courageously involves overcoming fear and worry, standing firm and with poise, and trusting God because we know in our hearts he is good and faithfully guides and protects us. As we take these steps to lead courageously we get to release the fullness of the Kingdom of Heaven here on earth into our area(s) of influence.

As a mother of three, I used to love watching my children play-acting when they were young. Their adventures were all about defeating an enemy and saving the world, they loved to be the superhero in every game. There was no fear or doubt, only certainty in their abilities driven by their imagination. They were confident in who they were and full of curiosity to venture into the unknown. They climbed trees, swung on ropes, jumped across mighty rivers (on one occasion one of my boys did not quite make it) and with never a second thought. When they bumped heads or fell to the ground, they would get up and do it all over again. As we move beyond childhood that courageous leadership spirit can get eroded. Life can beat us down, make us feel inferior and leave us feeling inadequate. We enter the world of adulthood looking through the lens of our (unique) belief system, which includes unhealthy lies and an awareness of the potential dangers in life, often subscribing to the doctrine of 'performance in order to achieve' to get approval. Before we know it our courage has gone and, with it, our ability to be a courageous leader. What people look for in a leader actually requires the leader to operate from a place of great courage.

Sadly, courageous leadership can be depicted as a 'tough boss' who, driven by their own worldly fears and anxieties, often resorts to taking actions that are authoritarian or dictatorial.

> Courageous leadership isn't about a title, position or status in society

...and it is most certainly not about leading by fear or control. It is about who you are: your character, your heart and your resilience. Kingdom-style leaders understand their calling to make the world a better place and confidently deliver what they have to offer the world. They are authentic and confident in who and what they believe and lead from a place of emotional maturity. They remain utterly dependent on God, maintaining fellowship with him so that it is his will done on earth. It is from this place of obedience they step out courageously.

The Vision
As we have previously discussed, for any leader, vision is essential. While any vision comes with doubt, the doubt must never be

allowed to paralyse the vision. Be clear about the vision God has given you and what you need to do to achieve the vision. Then step out courageously, making godly choices to bring the vision to fruition.

> Vision and courage go hand in hand with action.

At the opening of Disneyland, Florida, in 1971, someone is rumoured to have said to Walt Disney's widow, 'What a pity Walt didn't live to see this.' She replied, 'He did, that's why it's here!' Walt Disney famously said before he died, 'All our dreams can come true, if we have the courage to pursue them.' Courage insists on taking the first step. When you lead with courage, hesitation will be far from you and it feels so much better to move forward than to stand still and accomplish nothing.

> Boats are not designed to sit in the harbour looking decorative

...and we have not been created to just sit in a church when God has a clear vision and purpose for us beyond material walls. As Lord Chesterfield said, 'Man cannot discover new oceans unless he has the courage to lose sight of the shore.' There is no shame in altering the course of direction after the first step but we do need to set sail. It's possible to rationalise your way out of anything, so just make sure you are changing direction not out of fear but because God has spoken to you about a change of course. The problem with rationalisation is that it creates inaction; nothing ever gets accomplished when we can find all the reasons not to do something rather than looking at why action is needed. Procrastination and perfectionism are the two biggest wastes of time and neither have a place in Kingdom thinking. Focus on the mission and goals and, through intercession and prayer, find ways to get there instead of any reason not to try. There is no substitute for the first step; whatever the vision God has for you, go for it! *'The sovereign LORD is my strength; he makes my feet like the feet of a deer, he enables me to tread on the heights'* (Habakkuk 3:19).

Be True to Yourself

Jesus totally understood his mission and, from the security of knowing his identity, operated from approval rather than seeking approval from his father. From this stance he led courageously, even in his darkest hours to the cross. When you truly know your identity and your values and beliefs flow from this place, it becomes much easier to move forwards in the face of adversity rather than stand still or take a step back. As discussed in the previous chapters, relational leaders need to be aware of the negative thoughts in their minds and the emotions they activate that can deceive them into inappropriate compromise and avoidance. When you recognise such negative beliefs and expectations, redefine the belief to something that God believes of you and project this out to the world. Living with a belief that we are 'inadequate' goes against God's design that we are wonderfully made. Stand on truth and courageous leadership can flow.

Alongside standing true to godly values and behaviours, be aware of when your values differ from someone else's and how such differences can affect your responses.

I was raised with a 10-scoring trigger underpinned by 'always tell the truth'. When I know someone is lying, whether it is one of my children or someone in the work environment, I have to make a choice to not judge or attack but find a way to confront the issue whilst maintaining a healthy relationship with that person in an honouring way.

The ability to lead effectively through differences of opinion, ideas or perspectives is key to being a Kingdom-style leader. How we choose to handle people and situations when values and opinions differ to ours can affect all our relationships: at work, at home, at church and in our personal friendships. Learn how to deal with confrontation in a positive way, focusing on challenging the issue without compromising who you are as a person and without damaging the relationship you have with those involved.

I love how,

> Jesus was able to balance assertiveness
> and co-operation depending on the situation.

He instinctively knew when to be directive in his manner, to challenge and stand firm over something, but also when to encourage collaborative team working and bring compassion to the situation. He was able to be all these things because he listened to his Father's heart and responded from this place. Our heart is not just about emotions. As a spirit-filled leader our heart encompasses all our thoughts, insights and wisdom and is the dwelling place of the Holy Spirit. It is the very centre of who each of us is. Listen to what your heart tells you and discern with the Holy Spirit how to respond, keeping in check any negative thoughts and emotions before they have the chance to take control and impact negatively on a situation.

Secular and Sacred at All Times

Although many Christians live in countries that are tolerant to all spiritual backgrounds, many of us try to stash away our spirituality as we leave church on Sunday, rather than carry it with us into all areas of society for the rest of the week. We divide secular and sacred living when in reality they are inseparable to God. Our identity in Christ is who we are 24/7. We must not allow trends, popular opinion, or a louder voice to hold sway over what we truly know and believe in our heart. Spiritual strength is essential to establishing a firm moral foundation that cannot be blown over or toppled by the voices around us. Stay true to what you believe and stand firm in who you are.

> Ultimately, people notice there is something different about you, an inner peace and conviction that's attractive and they will choose to follow.

Learning how to stand firm is a bit like taking up membership at the gym. On your first visit you don't try to lift a bar full of heavy weights; you start with small ones and build your muscle by gradually adding more. Learn how to stand firm by taking incremental steps to project what's in your heart in order to connect with someone else's heart. Take an interest in them to understand what motivates them to take a particular approach. Share your perspective with the aim of moving forwards together. Protecting oneself from outside forces and influences is a natural reaction but we need to get to a place where our identity in God and self-confidence in who we are run deeper than self-protection.

I had a client storm into his first meeting with me and aggressively went on the attack as to why he thought the leadership development programme that was about to start was a waste of time and money. I knew that to match such agitation would only lead to an uncomfortable confrontation, so for 10 minutes, as the rant continued, I asked God, 'What is this all about, what's going on here?' because I wanted a Kingdom perspective to find a way to help him. As the tirade came to an end, prompted by the Holy Spirit, I courageously asked, 'What's this all about? This is not the real you; underneath this hard shell you are as soft as butter.' Anger melted into tears and he opened up about how a very difficult childhood had resulted in a learnt behaviour to protect himself and others when feeling threatened. The Peace and Comfort of God's Kingdom entered the room, and over the remainder of this meeting and the subsequent coaching sessions we unpacked the hurts of the past and began to rewrite his belief system. He has gone on to work at other organisations and has called upon my expertise as he continues to realise the benefits, particularly in his relationship with his children. God is so kind and always responds but he needs us to courageously and compassionately step out and go after the vision he has for other people's lives.

Jesus shows us how to stand out confidently rather than going into a self-protective mode, even when this made him vulnerable, and he did this because he knew it was the right thing to say or do.

> No true leader ever succeeded under a roof of self-protection.

When we put our head above the parapet and speak up we can do so knowing, as Jesus did, that Father God will support us. Jesus was good at reading situations but never caved in to opposition. He established trust by showing himself as human and recognising differences by showing empathy. He was authentic but skilful in navigating tricky pathways, taking people with him as he continued on mission. When I read the Gospels I appreciate how he took a stand with such compassion and empathy but was never blown around by prevailing earthly winds. His leadership is courageous to the core of who he is.

When to Step In

In the same way that people do not like an authoritarian, dictatorial leader, at the other end of the scale nobody likes a panicky, indecisive leader. Both extremes impact on the ability of others to trust such a leader. While any leader may have concerns that need to be addressed, how they handle such concerns says a lot about them. Bringing the peace of the Kingdom and keeping cool under pressure produces a calmness that spreads to those around, allowing everybody to think with a clear head and develop strategies that will bring people through any crisis. Think about Jesus' example when he calmed the storm; in contrast, the disciples decided to panic in the boat (Mark 4:35–41). Keep in mind, however, that poise without action is just as devastating as panic – it just takes longer to feel the results. Joshua 1:9 reminds us to *'Be strong and courageous. Do not be afraid; do not be discouraged, for the* LORD *your God will be with you wherever you go.'*

Fight the Fear

Courage is 'bravery' and the courage of one's convictions is 'to be brave enough to act in accordance with one's beliefs, no matter what the outcome'.[19] Most people have convictions, but many become too timid to take a stand when those convictions are challenged. To succeed as a courageous, Kingdom-style leader your convictions must overrule ungodly fear. In Deuteronomy 31:6 we read, *'Be strong and courageous. Do not be afraid or terrified because of them, for the* LORD *your God goes with you; he will never leave you nor forsake you.'* God obviously understands how susceptible we are to fear; with 'Fear not!' occurring more than 365 times it's the most repeated command in the Bible – more than one for every day of the year.

People who are courageous are not free from fear, they proceed despite the fear

...and do it anyway. Discipline and the willingness to say and do the things that no one else is prepared to do is courageous leadership; however, we need to learn how to say what needs to be said in an honouring way. Understanding some of the unhealthy beliefs you have unwittingly signed up to will help you walk through and away from the fear. Identify the lie you believe and laugh at it because it is a lie and no longer has power over you. Ask God for his forgiveness for believing the lie, renounce it and ask him to replace the lie with his truth. This positions you to push through whatever is holding you back. FEAR is simply an acronym for 'False Evidence Appearing Real'. Take it a step further and realise that often 'Fear is Fun in disguise!' Make a choice to risk standing for what you know in your heart is right regardless of the possible response. Leadership is a risk and the risk can be intellectual, emotional or spiritual. It feels like there is no safety in stepping up or stepping out when everybody else is just sitting around. If you effectively manage your emotional triggers and engage with the Holy Spirit to handle the situation, you are less likely to react out of fear, whether you are being silenced, are not being listened to or just need to take a stand and bring a different perspective. Often aggressive people attack to cover their insecurities so recognise this as an opportunity to love them. Keep your focus, remain calm and secure in who you are and seek God's presence. Keep honouring the person or group of people but stand firm and take the risk.

If we are to step out as courageous leaders we must alleviate the desire to focus on all the possible bad outcomes. About 80 per cent of worry is unfounded so we must manage our imagination so that it doesn't run wild.

> Worry is simply the wrong use of the imagination.

For me, growing up with a mum who worried about everything, the antidote to worry has been learning to become childlike with Father God. As his child we can live completely free from worry because not only is God in charge of everything but we have direct access to him. His love and protection keep us strong and worry free. To lead courageously, focus on all the great possibilities and dreams that God has shared with you for your life and courageously go after these knowing he is always there for you.

Trust

At the heart of courageous leadership is trust. It acts rather like the keel underneath a boat, keeping it upright. To illustrate trust in workshops I often hold up a piece of paper and ask the question, 'How long does it take to develop trust with another person?' The response is varied but illustrates a period of time. I then ask, 'How long does it take to destroy trust?' dramatically ripping the piece of paper in two. As I try to put the two pieces of paper back together I ask the final question, 'How long does it take to rebuild trust?' Of course, the answer to this question will vary and directly relates to the emotional maturity of the people involved. Trying to tape together the now two pieces of the paper may take years and the rip will always be visible. To totally rebuild trust requires both parties to agree to begin again with a fresh piece of paper, to 'forgive and let it go'. This takes great emotional maturity. It would be better not to break trust in the first place.

Trust develops from principles such as equity, compassion, integrity, justice and honesty that go far deeper than external factors such as gender, ethnicity, age and cultural barriers. We build trust by demonstrating respect, truly listening to people and seeking to understand. As we honour people and communicate their worth and value, they come to see and believe it in themselves. Honour helps to build a foundation of trust and from this place we are able to unleash the potential of the individual, team and organisation.

As Christians, trust needs to flow out from our relationship with God – from the inside, with intimacy before commission. If we don't trust our own convictions and beliefs, based on our relationship with God, this will affect the way we lead. The story of Gideon provides great lessons on this subject. Judges 6:12 states that *'When the angel of the Lord appeared to Gideon, he said, "The LORD is with you, mighty warrior."'* Gideon did not see himself as a courageous, mighty warrior but looked round to see who the angel was talking to. We all have our own Gideon moments! He doubted the Lord's commitment and saw only his own weakness, doubting that he was hearing from God. He became afraid of other people and needed reassurance but eventually, by trusting God, he became a courageous leader. Trusting God first opens the way to discerning with him how to develop trust around others.

Courage

Courageous Kingdom-style leaders utilise their knowledge, skills and experiences to achieve excellence in all they do and to engender this in everyone around them. Through emotional maturity, they are comfortable with admitting when they do not have all the answers and happily ask for support when required.

> Fear of failure and fear of rejection try to eat away at courageous leadership

...because they hide behind masks of control, perfectionism and procrastination. Kingdom-style leaders do not strive for perfectionism, as this will make anyone neurotic, but instead seek excellence in all they do. The mantra of 'What I have done is enough' prevents them falling into patterns of perfectionism and performance envy.

It is not possible to please everybody all the time but don't allow yourself or others to hold you back from achieving the vision you feel called to deliver because it is better to 'play it safe'. At a particularly challenging time in my life Father God showed me a picture of mountains and molehills. He creates mountains as treasure for us to conquer – that builds up our spiritual muscle and gives us a greater perspective, whereas Satan can only try and trip us up by building a little molehill. It makes me smile and reminds me whose Kingdom is majestic and all powerful. When faith is tested, it motivates us to trust God and pursue and draw closer to him and in these moments we get to conquer mountains. As we learn to conquer mountains with God it becomes so much easier to hurdle any molehills Satan throws our way. As courageous leaders we need to develop 'night vision' to enable us to see through the darkness around us, remembering God's promise in Isaiah 45:2–3: *'I will go before you and level the mountains; I will break down gates of bronze and cut through bars of iron. I will give you hidden treasures, riches stored in secret places, so that you may know that I am the* Lord.'

> When you feel out of your depth, know that God is there.

When you can't see and understand, trust your relationship with Jesus. I love the lyrics from Edward Mote's hymn of grace:

> When darkness seems to hide his face,
> I rest on his unchanging grace.
> When all around my soul gives way,
> He then is all my hope and stay.
> On Christ the solid rock I stand,
> All other ground is sinking sand.[20]

Spirit-filled, courageous leaders find ways to succeed by understanding who they are and how to lead relationally upwards, inwards and outwards, in a way that others choose to follow. As leaders, we all face trials and struggles and we need to learn how to overcome them in the face of adversity and uncertainty. We need the discipline to say no to anything that depletes and stops us growing and becoming who we are called to be. Courageous leadership is about putting ourselves out there, facing our fears, doubts and potential ridicule all for the greater good. While many people may not like what is required to become a courageous leader, very few regret what they have to go through to achieve it. It's time for godly sons and daughters to make a stand and lead by example as courageous leaders in order to bring his Kingdom in all its fullness.

Discussion and Activation

How do you relate to Gideon's story? Do you see yourself as a mighty warrior or doubt yourself?

To what extent does fear and worry stop you from being a courageous leader? What lies hold you back and how can you overcome them?

What courageous steps can you take to bring more of God's presence into your area(s) of influence?

Is there someone you can pray with to receive healing? Do you have a prophetic word that will encourage someone or a solution to a problem that God has given you?

Can you pray for Kingdom Peace, Comfort, Joy, Justice and Righteousness into a situation?

15
Optimistic Leader

Optimism is an essential quality in life. What I love about optimists is their excitement about the future and their energy that is so attractive to those around.

> Optimism is at the heart of courage

...because if we don't feel optimistic about tomorrow how can we find the courage to overcome any challenges today? Many people like to dismiss optimism as wishful thinking and daydreaming. They see optimism as some sort of psychological disorder exhibited by people who are out of touch with reality. Sadly, people who judge optimistic daydreamers are often, deep down, just envious of the kind of life such optimistic people lead: hopeful, happy and joyous. Somewhere along the way they experienced disappointment and don't want to hope again to avoid further hurt and pain. That's why we need to keep dealing with disappointment together with God because what we focus on can so easily become our reality. Whether you describe yourself as either a 'cup half full' or 'cup half empty' person, there is still half a cup of optimism missing and our attitude can affect our future.

As a Kingdom-style leader it can be dangerous to listen to another person who tells you to be 'realistic' when you share a dream, vision or prophetic word. Look what happened to Joseph when he shared with his family his dreams at a time when he and his brothers were emotionally immature and did not express themselves in the best way, though thankfully God had everything covered. Joseph is an example of how the world is changed by people who are labelled as out-of-touch daydreamers. World-changers are both good and evil but they share a common pattern of being able to imagine the possibilities and going on to shape history. As Kingdom-style leaders our opportunity is to bring the dreams and optimism of heaven here on earth based on godly truths even when evil and pessimism prowl our communities, towns, cities and nations. It's so easy to buy into the negativity being transmitted all around because rarely do we hear those reassuring words, 'Everything is going to be OK!' You only have to turn on the television or pick up a newspaper to be bombarded with pessimistic stories that affect the atmosphere over our nations across the world, whether financial, political or social stories. By the end of the day, if we allow ourselves to be influenced disproportionately by such doom and gloom, we head for bed feeling as though we've been on a rollercoaster of negative emotions. Society is manipulated by fear and pessimism, transmitted and hyped up by Satan, but as Christians we need to recognise that,

> what we see and hear may be based on facts but is not based on Kingdom reality.

There are negative things going on and bad things happen, but we need to learn to trust God, his Kingdom and how he is in control of all things past, present and future. As we shift our gaze upwards and live from the perspective of biblical truth that contains no pessimistic word in relation to the Kingdom, we get to live from a place of optimism. Lamentations 3:24–25 declares, *'I say to myself, "The Lord is my portion; therefore I will wait for* him." The LORD *is good to those whose hope is in him, to the one who seeks him.'*

We have all experienced what it is like to be around both optimistic and pessimistic people and, if we are honest, recognise our moments when we live in these opposite camps. Spending time with negative people is tiring as they suck your energy, like a vortex draining away everything good, and you come away feeling depleted. In a world where everything seems so bleak and news is communicated with a negative undertone,

> people look for leaders who radiate optimism and hope.

When you are around such people life feels good and the future looks brighter. Such leaders are encouragers and, like a magnet, you feel positively attracted towards their light because of their sunny disposition. If you want to become a Kingdom-style leader that people choose to follow, remember that optimism in leadership draws followers to you.

Repelling Pessimism

How we choose to respond to negativity around us often stems from what we are taught growing up. My dad often looked at life through a pessimistic rather than an optimistic lens. I also grew up with a 'scared' and emotionally fragile mum who saw only impossible mountains rather than conquerable molehills, so her lens was one of fear and anxiety. This combination meant I grew up in an atmosphere of emotional fear and pessimistic thinking in how to respond to people and situations around me. I have to be intentional in rewriting any belief that could take me to a similar place and catch myself to stop any negative thinking trying to creep back in.

By sensing the mood around you and recognising which

Kingdom you are tuning in to, every time Satan broadcasts his thoughts you can rise above his broadcast rather than being drowned out. As we intentionally spend intimate time with God and allow his Holy Spirit to fill us we get to live from a place of his optimism. His optimism becomes a part of our character and by positively positioning ourselves as we go about our daily life we are able to release God's Kingdom.

Stirred by the Holy Spirit I declared over one client that the year we were about to enter would be one of hope: the restoration of relationships and a bright new future. At her next coaching session she smiled as she told me that her Christmas present from her daughter was a ring with the inscription 'Hope' and this prophecy significantly impacted on both of us as I was able to share the Father's love for her as a cherished daughter. Although the year had its challenges, the client saw relationships improve and the year ended with hope. She has since invited Jesus into her life. More and more I am learning to stand in the gap of Kingdom Hope until hope gets restored into people's hearts.

Leading as an Optimist

Being an optimist may get you labelled as naive and a little crazy but it is the only stance that is truly reflective of God's Kingdom and character. Imagine the impact if visitors to church and those we work alongside met outrageous optimism every day and the impact such a stance might have as that atmosphere becomes part of how we 'do life' together? Growing up with a dad who was serious and often pessimistic in attitude, a big part of my journey has been learning that Father God is not only fun to be with, he is happy and in a good mood every day.

There was an occasion when I was shopping locally and asked God for clues to people he wanted to bless. I love God's sense of humour because his reply was a few lines from a nursery rhyme: 'Mary, Mary quite contrary, how does your garden grow? . . . And pretty maids all in a row.' With this one clue I started to look for 'pretty maids all in a row' and to my surprise found three little elderly ladies standing next to each other, one of which was wearing a dressing-up hat shaped like a flower, which made me smile. I approached her and asked, 'Is your name Mary by any chance?' to which she replied, 'Yes, why do you ask?' I explained that I am a Christian who believes that God likes to speak through us and asked if there was anything I could pray that would bless her? Her response was, 'I've been to mass today so I don't think so, but it's lovely to know he is thinking about me today,' and with that she disappeared to catch her bus.

God is very optimistic and sits on his throne smiling and singing over us. He wants his children to be the same and to bring about an optimistic cultural shift. If being an optimist sparks questions in others, this brings the opportunity to open up discussion and create positive change. Such an approach will be challenged when you come up against a pessimist because pessimism is rooted in lies and comes from Satan. It's important that we learn to navigate the difficult waters of pessimism because that way, as we radiate optimism, there is hope that pessimists will catch a revelation from the Holy Spirit, which brings life to them.

My dad would have defined himself not as a pessimist but as a realist because, like many others, he operated on the model of sin at one end of a scale and holiness at the other, with a middle ground called 'realism'. We try to justify ourselves sitting in the middle because whilst we are not perfect we are trying our best. God sees this very differently. His position is black or white, light or darkness, good or evil, optimism or pessimism. If you don't think like an optimist, then you are responding as a pessimist. Convincing ourselves it is OK to sit in the middle is simply trying to justify our position, based on the lie that this does not offend anyone. However, it offends God because it does not reflect his hope for us to be optimists. Trying to mix black and white makes grey and we lose the colour and vibrancy of heaven in our life. As I've grappled with this either/or revelation, I thought I'd look up the definition of 'realistic'; interestingly, it states: 'showing awareness or acceptance of things as they really are'.[21] This definition raises the question, what is reality? Here are a few other words that describe aspects of being realistic, but hear them through God's lens: practical, down-to-earth, sensible, commonsensical, level-headed, clear-sighted, achievable, within the bounds of possibility, viable, reasonable, doable, and I particularly like this phrase, 'both feet on the ground'. As I perused these, I felt God whisper in my ear, 'Who does this remind you of?' and immediately I knew they reminded me of Jesus. Kingdom-style leaders,

> walk on earth from a place of outrageous optimism based on practical, clear-sighted, Kingdom reality and possibilities.

Right now you may be walking through very tough times and I don't want to diminish the challenges that you are facing. The optimistic truth of the Kingdom is that God always has a rescue plan and is at hand even if right now you feel like you can't get to the other side. If we are going to behave like Jesus we need to shift our thinking to one of positivity and optimism. We previously explored that a Kingdom-style leader understands that you can't be an optimist whilst living in a place of hopelessness, because hopelessness says 'What's the point, it's not going to work'. Proverbs 13:12 teaches us that *'hope deferred makes the heart sick'*. Hope brings strength and peace because it comes from the truth that God is in charge and, through his abundant love, he has everything covered.

Optimists explore their dreams whereas pessimists shut them down because they are just fantasy or potential nightmares.

Optimistic leaders exude hope and wait patiently for things to work through according to God's Plan A, resting in the truth that he is in charge. There is power in thinking and speaking optimistically from a Kingdom perspective over all situations, however challenging they appear. Pessimists become impatient and lethargic basing everything on what can be seen that brings a negative attitude of 'What's the point, it's not going to work, I'll leave it to others.'

Optimists expend all their energy on building up, encouraging and honouring others because they choose to see them as God sees them, whether they are partners, family, work colleagues, bosses, church leaders, politicians or their home nation. In contrast, pessimists can be unrelenting in their judgements of themselves and other people's faults and failures and find it hard to forgive.

Optimists sing and laugh from an overflow of the joy of the Kingdom, whereas pessimists find it hard to laugh and end up silenced by others because they are so negative and hard work to be around. To paraphrase George Müller – a man responsible for the care of 10,000 orphans, who established 117 schools and travelled more than 100,00 miles preaching the gospel – 'My first job in the morning is to get joyful with God.'[22]

The Courage of Conviction

We explored earlier the story of Nehemiah as a demonstration of servant leadership but he was also an optimistic, hope-filled leader and demonstrated how to overcome the worst barrage of pessimism in the character of Sanballat. Nehemiah was devastated when he witnessed what had happened to Jerusalem and wept, mourned, prayed and fasted as a way of processing where he was emotionally. He also knew the truth of who God is and, because God mattered to him, chose to rebuild Jerusalem from the rubble in order to glorify him. His opposition came in the person of Sanballat who, fuelled by his own insecurities, anger and rage, stood on the sidelines mocking, threatening, causing riots and confusion and accusations against Nehemiah to try and create an atmosphere of fear and failure. Nehemiah, through prayer, wisdom and trusting God, remained optimistic and carried on rebuilding.

Part of our challenge is that we will also face Sanballat-type characters in our area(s) of influence. Pessimists behave like a dog with a bone, relentlessly clinging on to their negative 'It's not going to work' attitude to try and exhaust any optimist. Nehemiah did not buy in to Sanballat's barrage of lies, however hard and demeaning they became. When we face such an assault it is so tempting to crumble because it feels like the only defence is to change who we are and to stop what we are doing. As a pessimist finds themselves cornered they fight back harder, resorting to further deception. Such a barrage is uncomfortable and unpleasant for those around and isolates them as they seek allies to invest into their 'conflict'.

The Kingdom is all about fellowship, the body working together as one, but pessimists struggle to connect with others and God because they are right and everyone else, including God, must therefore be wrong. Nehemiah did not buy into fear that could have resulted in him giving up, but continued to move forwards, making it harder for pessimistic Sanballat to catch up. As a pessimist becomes more selfish, self-centred and unable to give to others, their fears and concerns block the road forwards in contrast to optimists who work as a team, removing any obstacles and building momentum until their work is complete.

Reasons to be Cheerful

As optimists we get to fight for our family, friends and work colleagues from a place of identity and not from the small world of 'me, me, me'.

> The optimist knows it's all about God, walking by the Spirit and trusting in God's plans and purposes.

Even when we know this in our hearts, there are times when we struggle to stay in an optimistic place. This is when it can be helpful to review the list of things that you are grateful for that we looked at as part of being a relational leader. Here are a few of mine that may help you get started with your own list:

- I know I am unconditionally loved by Father God and he smiles and sings over me not for what I achieve but for who I am: his beloved daughter.
- God's Plan A is happening today even if it doesn't feel like it. *"'They will fight against you but will not overcome you, for I am with you and will rescue you," declares the LORD'* (Jeremiah 1:19).
- Today is a day Father God and I can have fun together and I can rely on him to help me through my challenges.
- There is an abundant banqueting feast laid out before me today that goes way beyond what I need. I have an extravagant Father.

- I've read the last chapter in the Bible so I know I am on the side that has won. I am seated in the heavenly place whatever the situation and circumstance.
- I can enjoy sunrise and sunsets knowing that God's Son rose for me. His creation and beauty is all around reminding me who he is.

Kingdom-style leaders who operate from a position of optimism have many advantages over any pessimist. Think about it, who would you rather go to for wisdom and discernment, an optimist or a pessimist? An optimist sees opportunity where others see uncertainty and despair. As Winston Churchill is reported to have said, 'Optimists see opportunities in every difficulty.' They problem-solve by facing obstacles head on, analysing them and formulating solutions that lead people forwards. They also problem solve from a perspective of improving a situation rather than trying to deny, avoid and distort the problem, dwelling on their negative feelings. Optimistic leaders are more resilient in the face of challenges and setbacks.

> Optimists see failure as a chance to learn and grow.

When fear of failure couples with pessimism both the leader and the followers are held back.

We need to become leaders who are resilient, able to adapt to setbacks, get everyone back on track and keep moving forwards. This is what sets an optimistic leader apart from a pessimistic leader. An optimist is capable of fully understanding the risks but can mitigate against those risks with an optimistic rather than a pessimistic approach. Such optimistic confidence that everything is going to work out OK sustains a positive mood that helps team morale and enhances their prospects of success. When action is needed, optimism, even if perceived as a little crazy, can be a good thing.

Optimism in leaders is infectious and can lead to the spread of more optimism by followers. The impact of a leader's outlook, whether optimistic or pessimistic, will spread to others they come into contact with both at work or when they go home. We can all cite examples of having to follow a leader whose mood swings impact the tone for the day. As they arrive you observe the atmosphere around them to assess whether today is going to be positive or negative. Their mood is infectious and will suppress or lift the atmosphere across the workplace, which in turn impacts productivity and morale. Sadly, when such a leader goes home their mood is also gauged by family members, and an appropriate coping strategy is adopted dependent on how angry or happy the individual is that evening. There is a difference between being real with how we feel (and learning how to safely deal with our triggers) and allowing our negativity and mood to impact those around us. If we,

> set the tone to be happy and optimistic, those around us are more likely to become happier.

Humans tend to seek to hang out with others having a similar emotional behaviour. A final thought by Winston Churchill: 'A pessimist sees the difficulty in every opportunity; an optimist the opportunity in every difficulty.' Optimists see the big picture and help those around them to see beyond their most recent experiences and into a better future. Kingdom-style optimists paint the eternal picture and bring people into that place. The good news is that optimistic leaders are inspiring communicators, which is great news because you cannot elicit enthusiasm for an idea unless you're a strong communicator.

Discussion and Activation

How do others see you in terms of being an optimist or pessimist? How can you nurture your expression of being optimistic?

Who are your Sanballats in your area(s) of influence and what have you learnt in how to handle these relationships effectively?

When are you a Sanballat? What do you need to work on in order to become an optimist?

List your reasons to be a grateful optimist and then declare them over yourself (and to the group).

16
Influencing Leader: Shifting Atmospheres

There is one particular passage in the Bible that has started to make me think beyond even courageous and optimistic leadership, particularly when considering the strife in the world around us reported on a daily basis – the 'armour of God' in Ephesians (6:10–13):

Finally, be strong in the Lord and in his mighty power. Put on the full armour of God, so that you can take your stand against the devil's schemes. For our struggle is not against flesh and blood, but against the rulers, against the authorities, against the powers of this dark world and against the spiritual forces of evil in the heavenly realms. Therefore put on the full armour of God, so that when the day of evil comes, you may be able to stand your ground, and after you have done everything, to stand.

This scripture talks about our struggle not being against flesh and blood but external evil forces around us: rulers, authorities and powers of darkness. If we can change our emotional intelligence by taking authority over the battle in our minds can we also influence these negative, external spiritual forces circling us? Can we learn how to recognise and take authority over them, radically changing not only the resonance and harmony of our relationships with family, friends and work colleagues but also over our towns, cities and across the globe? Can we become leaders who influence culture through shifting atmospheres?

Atmospheres and How to Recognise Them

An atmosphere is a dynamic that influences the way we think, behave and respond to God and/or the world and other forces around us. Have you ever walked into a room feeling happy and for no obvious reason suddenly started to feel overwhelmingly sad, like you want to burst into tears? This is an example of how you can pick up an atmosphere in a room that is not 'your stuff' and it can really impact on how you feel and react.

Consider the effect music has when you watch a film.

As a teenager, I went with a group of friends to see the first *Friday the 13th*[22] film (before I realised that going to such films was not such a good idea!). All of us entered the cinema with the attitude of 'nothing scares me' but from the first frightening scene, exacerbated by the music and sound effects, *everyone* was screaming and I ended up jumping out of my skin, with popcorn going everywhere.

The movie industry goes to great lengths to manipulate our emotions: to scare us or to make us feel sad, happy or to cry.

The truth is that we are in a spiritual battle with Satan transmitting his negativity, which we pick up, consciously or subconsciously. We then create and react to the atmospheres and, with no reference point for such transmitted atmospheres, we end up getting caught in and manoeuvred by them along with everyone else. What if we could enable an atmosphere in our areas of influence and, like a thermostat, change atmospheric temperatures towards heaven rather than matching its level like a thermometer? This could make a huge difference to those affected, perhaps even between life and death.

In the 'Relational Leader' chapters we explored the importance of recognising and dealing with the chatterbox lies transmitted by Satan. However, there are times when the lies picked up are not 'my stuff'; we are simply sensing what Satan is depositing into the atmosphere which we can begin to partner with if we are not on our guard. Shifting atmospheres is about being attuned to your environment and recognising which Kingdom you are tuning in to, and making the choice to remain with Jesus.

We all need to learn not to get tossed around by negativity in our internal thinking and external atmospheres but remain an optimist. From that place we can take authority over misleading atmospheres such as fear and hopelessness and release God's Kingdom of Joy, Peace, Comfort, Salvation and Deliverance, Healing, Justice and God's presence into the situation. Remember,

> the reality that you believe in will be the one you transmit.

God's ability to change atmospheres is limitless if we only recognise this and partner with him.

One assignment, I was asked to work with two teams that had originally been part of two different organisations that had merged. Together, the two 'camps' had become dysfunctional because they were culturally very different. Tensions were high as, inevitably, were inappropriate behaviours. I visited both teams separately and carried out various exercises to explore their cultures and how they felt about each other, which resulted in very unhappy reading. The task was to facilitate a day's workshop to bring about some sort of miraculous solution. Armed with some ideas on how to run the day I prayed as I drove to the venue. God began to share a 'once upon a time story' that he said would enlighten both parties and help them move forward. The story included characters such as the lord of the manor, a knight in shining armour,

Friar Tuck, a duchess and a fairy godmother. With nothing better, I made the decision to run with this rather crazy solution. I knew there was one Christian attending and smiled as I realised he was parked in the car next to me as I drove in. I explained that I needed prayer cover for this particular exercise to combat anything ungodly, and in we went. The atmosphere in the room was one of passive–aggressive resentment and hopelessness but I refused to be affected by this and began to project the opposite. The 'once upon a time' story began to unfold and with it the atmosphere began to shift towards acceptance, unity and hope (my intercessor did a fantastic job). At the coffee break afterwards the senior director exclaimed, 'I don't know how you did that but something has changed and I think it worked!'

Recognising Unwelcome Atmospheres

Proverbs 25:28 warns us, *'Like a city whose walls are broken through is a person who lacks self-control.'* Part of such self-control is learning how to rule our spirit so that we can influence the culture around us via shifting atmospheres. To be able to shift an atmosphere you must first recognise how you identify one, tuning in to what you feel, hear, sense and see:

Has how you are FEELING suddenly changed for no obvious reason?
Are you HEARING other voices? (i.e. Satan's agenda)
Do OBJECTS make you feel negative?
Are you seeing PICTURES in your mind that are not part of your normal thoughts?

Learn to recognise when you have picked up an atmosphere and your spirit has been shifted in a way you are not happy with. The physical environment reflects the spiritual world; if somewhere feels unsafe to you it probably is unsafe.

I once took a wrong turn ending up in a very run-down, inner-city area that I was unfamiliar with and suddenly began to feel fear and apprehension. An inner voice was saying a number of negative things that were not my normal pattern of thinking and it felt dark and unsafe. Thankfully, I recognised what I was sensing and began to pray for protection, Peace and God's presence into the area as I continued to drive through and the negative feeling dissipated as I continued to pray.

One way to familiarise yourself with the patterns around atmospheres is to record, in a journal, what you are picking up, whether in your church, workplace, shopping centre, school gates and any other places you visit. (My children quickly identify when I come under the influence of the atmosphere I feel in a certain chain of stores, as I become very grumpy!)

Taking 'My Stuff' Out of the Equation

As well as being aware of how we pick up atmospheres we need to manage 'my stuff' (discussed in the 'Relational Leader' chapters). We can hear three voices in our head: our 'self-talk', the chatterbox back-seat driver (Satan) and God. By cleaning up the chatterbox voice and your 'self-talk', you can discern atmospheres without 'my stuff' getting in the way. Regularly ask yourself, 'How am I doing?', 'Am I feeling good or not?' It is so easy to allow our 'self-talk' to join with Satan's voice to the point that we find it hard to differentiate them. But the truth is that God corrects but never condemns. He continues to unconditionally love us even when we mess up and he never plays the shame game. Any condemning talk means we are tapping into the wrong realm and partnering with Satan's lies. Keeping healthy and well-balanced physically, emotionally and spiritually, and allocating time at rest with God will enable you to discern what is happening around you. By being overtired, stressed, feeling unwell and generally out of balance you risk becoming more vulnerable to negative 'self-talk' and succumbing to influence by negative atmospheres. Have a compelling vision for your development and model your life on it, e.g. time with God, dealing with sin, preaching by actions not words, being authentic with character and heart issues, giving permission to others to speak into your life so that Satan can't eat away at you. At the end of each day, be honest with God so that your sin does not impact on tomorrow. This way, when you pick up an atmosphere you'll know it's not 'my stuff' and how to be true to yourself. Have integrity around who you are to enable you to guard against deceit in your heart. Check up on yourself by regularly asking:

> 'Is my imagery of me better than I really am?',
> 'Am I dealing with my inner voice and junk?'

If you are giving input into other people's lives you need to be open yourself. Things that are familiar to you will not necessarily be discerned as quickly as the things that are not part of your pattern of thinking. It is so easy to partner with the familiar without even realising because the pattern can feel normal. Before you know it you have come under it.

For me, having grown up in a family that had an 'always work hard and try your best' ethic, I can easily come under the 'hard work never kills' atmosphere. This will result in overworking because I am buying into the lie that everything must be done perfectly rather than recognising what I have done is enough and it's time to rest.

This is why it is important to,

> allow godly brothers and sisters around you
> to discern for you the things you do not see yourself.

Build relationships that teach you how to care for each other in this way. Ephesians 1:18–19 allows for this: *'I pray that the eyes of your heart may be enlightened in order that you may know the hope to which he has called you, the riches of his glorious inheritance in his holy people, and his incomparably great power for us who believe.'*

Using the Armour of God

Recognise your Ephesians 6 opportunities, dressed in the armour of God. Our response to Satan's broadcast needs to be, 'Now I see you, your time is up!' Often when I walk into client offices, particularly in London, I will pick up combinations of heaviness, fear and a sense of isolation, entitlement and hopelessness. I recognise those feelings were not there when I left home. Such an atmosphere is a reflection of the negative culture of the organisation and the way they go about their business unknowingly in partnership with Satan's world; partnering with this would result in me behaving in the same way. Instead, I choose to take authority over it, outrageously and optimistically bringing the opposite, using particularly hope, joy, generosity and acceptance.

There was one particular office where I would pick up an atmosphere of heaviness to do with characteristics of high performance and isolation that felt unhealthy as I walked in. The poor receptionist always looked like she had the weight of the world on her shoulders as people talked down to her in a very dishonouring way. I felt God say one morning that I should buy some daffodils, give them to her and encourage her through declaring her value and the outstanding job that she was doing. It was such fun to see her begin to smile in disbelief as the atmosphere changed around her. I continued on this theme throughout the day, lavishing encouragement and generosity as I met those I was coaching.

'Be strong in the Lord and in his mighty power. Put on the full armour of God, so that you can take your stand against the devil's schemes' (Ephesians 6:10–11). Wearing the full armour of God you can confidently stand firm because you are on the side that has already won because with God you can discern the difference between good and evil. You are righteousness so whatever darkness comes towards you do not partner with it but instead release the righteousness of Jesus. Ask yourself,

'What is Jesus saying and wanting me to do here?'

Be alert but not alarmed and learn to be a thermostat for the atmosphere, shifting the controls positively rather than complying with any negativity.

Many years ago my daughter was taking several dance exams and, as I sat in the corner quietly reading a book, I became aware of an atmosphere shift in the room as one after another the women kept making negative comments about their husbands and partners. The room went darker and darker. Not wanting to accede to this atmosphere of dishonour and hopelessness, I started to pray quietly and then entered the conversation with a positive statement about my husband. Instantly, another mum made a similar positive statement about her partner and the others followed suit. I could feel the atmosphere shifting as the room became brighter.

Hebrews 5:14 explains, *'But solid food is for the mature, who by constant use have trained themselves to distinguish good from evil.'* This is good news because we can train our senses against good and evil without having to worry about getting it right first time. In your area(s) of influence you will regularly get invited into people's atmospheres and it is important not to acknowledge or let in what they bring with them. If you don't take the opportunities to practise discerning the status of your immediate atmosphere, you can easily conclude that they and the world are too messed up and you can't help them. Even in church settings, be aware that some people who have received healing prayer are healed but still believe they are not because they hang on to the atmosphere around them. The solution is for them to stop partnering with it by standing on truth and releasing their healed self into the atmosphere.

As I began coaching a senior manager, she began to share a catalogue of difficult challenges she had faced over the past decade that concluded with a statement that her 'life was hopeless'. Of course my first response was not to partner with her hopelessness because I knew it was a lie. The truth is that God has a plan for her life and there is always hope. To her surprise I openly began to declare this at the first meeting saying that, though I recognised she had walked through a very dark valley, I did not believe her life was hopeless and that over the coming months my desire was to see hope restored. Though she lacked belief I stood in the gap and continued to declare, continuously praying until gradually glimmers of hope appeared.

I am actually beginning to enjoy warring Satan because I know his time is up! When I recognise an atmosphere that needs changing, I remember I have the authority to come against it by calling down God's Kingdom. When we get to declare the goodness of God, Satan's only option is to flee.

Practicalities of Shifting Atmospheres

There are a number of practical ways to shift atmospheres. Through *worship and praise* because this keeps our focus on God's heavenly Kingdom. Don't allow Satan to take advantage and instead go on the offensive through radical worship. Keep worshipping to allow your spirit to be expressed. Don't wait for freedom before you worship but worship until freedom comes. Remembering who God is leads us to worship and worship leads us to communion with him. In this intimate place he then reveals the Glory and, as we stand in the Glory, atmospheres shift. Worship and a Kingdom perspective keep us in a place of joy and contentment because we worship the one we love who, in turn, shifts the atmosphere and in that place of worship and thanksgiving Satan has no foothold.

We can shift atmospheres through *prayer and intercession*. Never underestimate the power of prayer in your work environment or local neighbourhoods so that you can hear, sense and feel God's heart for his people. Really concentrate on tuning in and don't dismiss thoughts as being just your imagination. Our imagination comes from God and you just need to discern whether you are connecting to God's voice or the lies of Satan that like to partner with our negative 'self-talk'. As we capture and dismiss the chatterbox voice we get to focus and act on what God is saying. Tune in to his Kingdom, recognising what is sealed in the heavenly realms and pray from that place, not from an earthbound perspective. God is God. He is good all the time. Praying allows the Spirit to enter in. As you pray you can start to feel the atmosphere shift because God always responds. As an atmosphere sensor, I can become overwhelmed with needing to do something all the time; this will kick in as over-responsibility if I am not managing 'my stuff'. What I am learning is that although we learn to discern an atmosphere, we do not necessarily have to take authority over it. Ask God if he wants you to do something about it or just not be influenced by it. Remember, always intercede from the place of love as Jesus taught us in John 17:23: *'you . . . have loved them even as you have loved me'*. Our intercession should never come over as judgemental and dishonouring.

Recognise the power of *prophetic actions* alongside intercession. This can be great fun but also makes a significant difference. Consider releasing balloons over an area with Bible quotes attached to bring down heaven. Dancing and singing are great ways to shift atmospheres.

We held a women's conference at church several years ago and through worship I became aware of an atmosphere of fear in the room. So I went to the back of the hall and, along with several other intercessors, began dancing. The band led us into a song about freedom and chains being removed and these words became a declaration in the room. As people sang and began to dance you could feel the atmosphere shift and Freedom and Joy began to touch everyone. It was incredible and led so very sensitively by the worship leader.

Another prophetic action is the use of bells as a way to call people to worship. The ringing of the church bells was introduced as a way of calling people into church at the right time.

The use of *declarations* is another effective way to shift

atmospheres and are powerful weapons. Pray and declare God's truth for restoration over homes, streets, neighbourhoods, your workplace or at the school gate. Declare prosperity, revival, fertile soil (people saved), encouragement and hope.

> I worked part time at a hospital over an eight-month period and regularly took the opportunity to walk around the outpatient clinics quietly praying and declaring 'your Kingdom come', particularly calling down Peace, Healing and Comfort. I was amused to hear that a 'secret shopper' had completed a feedback sheet and written that 'Outpatients felt very peaceful'.

What a privilege to be able to partner with God in so many ways. It is incredible that we get to impact on the world around us, rather than the other way around. Let's learn to take a position from a Kingdom perspective as Kingdom-style leaders so that we can influence culture through shifting atmospheres.

Discussion and Activation

How do you pick up atmospheres? What next steps can you take to develop your ability to pick up atmospheres?

How good are you at recognising 'your stuff'? Do you keep yourself balanced physically, emotional and spiritually? What are familiar patterns of thinking that you may need others to help you re-examine? (Refer to the 'Relational Leader' chapter on maturing emotional intelligence.)

Identify an example of when you discerned an atmosphere. Did you recognise what was going on or were you influenced by it? What might you do differently next time?

What practical ways (worship, intercession, prophetic actions, declarations) can you proactively act to shift atmospheres?

What has been apparent to you in regard to shifting atmospheres? What steps can you take to develop in this area?

17
It's Time to Influence: Step Up and Step Out

The early church described in the book of Acts was full of Kingdom-style leaders who not only recognised that Christ was real but took action because they knew he was powerful and had changed everything. Against great opposition and suffering, the gospel message spread quickly as his radical followers, like an army advancing, made ground. Acts 17:6 (NKJV) describes how these leaders were met with the cry: *'These who have turned the world upside down have come here too.'* Such men and women were visible, vibrant, militant followers of Jesus who shook and shaped the advance of Christianity in its early years. We have the same calling as these early believers to *'go and make disciples of all nations'* (Matthew 28:19). We are called to take our faith beyond the confines of the church into our daily lives, wherever we are called to influence. God's plan goes beyond just earning a living: wanting us to grow and reproduce, make disciples, and release his Kingdom to transform society to reflect heaven.

As Kingdom ambassadors there is an opportunity to catch God's vision that,

> our 'work' is the mission we are called to influence

…described in Colossians 3:23: *'Whatever you do, work at it with all your heart, as working for the Lord, not for human masters'.* Jesus carried out his ministry on the road, eating and working with his disciples and intentionally interacting with them as they experienced life together. He showed how to take people as you find them and walk with them as they take steps forwards. Whether in a prominent leadership role or simply carrying the mindset of Kingdom leadership God has sent you to love, value, equip, encourage and release those you encounter in your area(s) of influence through covert and overt operations. It's time for every Christian to recognise who they are as an adopted, beloved child of God and walk with such Kingdom authority that every area of society is transformed to reflect *'on earth as it is in heaven'*.

Professional athletes know the importance of running their own race and alongside their coach tailor a plan for each competition to avoid being influenced by anyone else's tactics. God has provided a personalised plan for each of us to run, described in Jeremiah 29:11, *"'I know the plans I have for you," declares the* LORD. *"Plans to prosper you and not to harm you, plans to give you hope and a future.'"* Sometimes it feels like we are in a sprint race and other times a marathon and there are also periods when we can't race and need to rest as God heals us physically, emotionally and spiritually. Whichever season of life you are in, remain resilient and focused and allow God to continue to develop your character, gifting and experiences so that you run in a way that glorifies him. As God's sons and daughters we are called to run this race together, encouraging one another to produce our personal best as we transform society.

To equip his people for works of service, so that the body of Christ may be built up until we all reach unity in the faith and in the knowledge of the Son of God and become mature, attaining to the whole measure of the fullness of Christ.

Then we will no longer be infants, tossed back and forth by the waves, and blown here and there by every wind of teaching and by the cunning and craftiness of people in their deceitful scheming.

Instead, speaking the truth in love, we will grow to become in every respect the mature body of him who is the head, that is, Christ. From him the whole body, joined and held together by every supporting ligament, grows and builds itself up in love, as each part does its work. (Ephesians 4:12–16)

Living this way requires us to love and respect one another as we participate in the ultimate race, passing the baton between each other and from generation to generation as one.

I coach many leaders who do not yet know Jesus and that's OK because he will save them when the time is right. What I am convinced about is that when they catch a glimpse of God's love and Kingdom-style leadership and like what they see, they make the choice to lead in this way. As they begin to demonstrate a new way of working, the culture around them begins to be transformed for those they are privileged to lead. As each leader begins to operate from more of a Kingdom perspective, like a snowball effect, others around learn to do the same. The snowball gets bigger and rolls faster, eventually causing an avalanche that impacts on not just the immediate team but an entire department and even an entire organisation.

I saw one such snowball effect in a client who, after detaching herself from negative lies that had held her back, summarised her key learning with the statement, 'Would it be too profound to say that for the first time I have found peace?' From this place of truth she led her team in a very different way, with positive feedback from her followers, peers and boss.

Let's recognise our call to influence, learn how to be a Kingdom-style leader and go on to raise those around us as Kingdom-style leaders so that society begins to reflect more of heaven on earth. As we go after cultural transformation let's keep celebrating God's goodness and being grateful for all he has done alongside giving thanks as Jesus continues to save people and build his Church. This is the partnership God is looking for.

In Matthew 14 there is the story of how the disciples were startled to see Jesus walking on water but he told them not to be afraid. Peter asked Jesus if he could join him on the water and, fixing his eyes on him, took a step out of the boat. When he took his eyes off Jesus and focused on the storm around him he became afraid and began to sink, calling out to Jesus for help. It is easy to allow ourselves to see Peter's story as a failure but he was the only disciple with the courage, conviction of faith and total trust in Jesus that enabled him to get out of the boat.

> No other disciple experienced what it was like to walk on water.

Faith can be frightening but we must remain obedient and, figuratively speaking, get out of our boats. The good news is that faith increases when we exercise it and it produces greater humility, boldness and obedience. It's time to step out in faith with our sails catching the wind of the Holy Spirit because that way we will see God in action. God seeks sons and daughters who are prepared to get out of their boat, keep their eyes fixed on Jesus and walk on water, following him into every area of influence and depositing his Kingdom influence wherever they go. Just being present with God, miracles can happen – if we stay obedient, humble and courageous.

Restoration across all of the world's nations will not happen if we remain safely in our church. By doing this we miss the reality that God is an extraordinary, consuming fire who could wipe out the entire planet as we could choose to squash a bug. We must not downsize God to fit our domesticated picture of him or our own insecurities. This is not God's desire and there is a call on church leadership to raise disciples and release apostolic and prophetic leaders (in the workplace as much as anywhere else) and the people of God so that they can run free to prepare for the return of the King. The last question the disciples asked Jesus, recorded in Acts 1:6–8, was:

'Lord, are you at this time going to restore the kingdom to Israel?' He said to them: 'It is not for you to know the time or dates the Father has set by his own authority. But you will receive power when the Holy Spirit comes on you; and you will be my witnesses in Jerusalem, and in all Judea and Samaria, and to the ends of the earth.

It's time to mobilise, declaring God's will and purpose that:

The earth will be filled with the knowledge of the glory of the LORD *as the waters cover the sea.* (Habakkuk 2:14)

Revival was not meant to start from scratch with each generation. The intention was for each generation to leave an inheritance (their ceiling) for the next generation to build on (their floor) and keep building. Sadly, we have had a cycle of revival but the baton has not been passed on so each generation has to start again. We need to have a lasting influence and pass the baton to the next generation so that new territories brought to God will never again be inhabited by Satan.

> What will be your ceiling that you pass on to
> the next generation for them to stand on as their floor?

Will it be the pupils you teach, the clinical staff you support or the children you raise? Will it be the next generation of managers in business or up-and-coming politicians, scientists, artists or journalists? Pass the baton so that God's Kingdom will continue to advance in preparation for Jesus' return.

God is passionately interested in the workplace and is moving his children out into all areas of society. Whether you are apostolic, a prophet, evangelist, pastor or teacher, don't limit your thinking to only the church environment but allow your gifts to be used in your area(s) of influence. It's time for a paradigm shift, to raise workplace Kingdom-style leaders to claim back ground for Jesus – in hospitals, homes, businesses, schools, the media, local and central government, arts, science and technology, the criminal justice system and so on.

> Whatever you do, go out as a Kingdom-style leader
> and be the best you can be for God.

Wherever you work, allow Jesus to take the lead and follow him as you walk together. When our calling and gifting come together as the body of Christ and we all *go and make disciples of all nations,* the result will shake the status quo to its foundations. It will be like an invasion of heaven on earth.

I want to finish with Psalm 1:1–3, which I have heard referenced as the 'businessman's psalm' but equally applies across all the areas of influence:

Blessed is the one who does not walk in step with the wicked or stand in the way that sinners take or sit in the company of mockers, but whose delight is in the law of the LORD, and who meditates on his law day and night. That person is like a tree planted by streams of water, which yields its fruit in season and whose leaf does not wither – whatever they do prospers.

Discussion and Activation

What has been your key learning from this book? What has impacted you the most?

What steps are you going to take to bring greater Kingdom-style influence in your area(s) of influence?

Who have you identified to help you keep on track? Who will be your encourager who can also hold you accountable?

Summary: Prophetic Word 'Called to Influence'

My journey to understand my personal call to influence came out of a prophecy received in 2007 and it is this prophecy, documented below, that began my quest to seek a different approach. It feels fitting to include it at the end of this book as an encouragement to you.

Making Your Mark

I know that you want to make your mark, setting the surrounding area ablaze. I am going to show you how to do this. For making your mark will not come from building bricks and mortar and you do not want to be remembered for this. Making your mark will come from the impression you leave on people's hearts. This is what you want to be remembered for. Be known as a generation who loved Jesus and displayed his love for the world to all those around regardless of who they are. To make your mark you will need to be lateral not literal thinkers and shapers. Do not be of this world, but live from a Kingdom perspective. I am the Kingdom, the Power and the Glory for ever and ever.

> 'You are the light of the world. A town built on a hill cannot be hidden. Neither do people light a lamp and put it under a bowl. Instead they put it on its stand, and it gives light to everyone in the house. In the same way, let your light shine before others, that they may see your good deeds and praise your Father in heaven' (Matthew 5:14–16).

I have given you a blueprint for my house. What it should look like on the inside and on the outside. See that I have given you, through my Word, firm foundations on which to build. Keep rooted on these foundations, encouraging each other and standing firm to the truth. See that I have placed you together to be Church. Each of you has your own skills and talents, and together you make the body of Christ. Use your talents wisely and work together for the good of the entire body, and do not let differences stand in the way. Remember at all times to be led not by your power and might but by the power of the Holy Spirit. Submit to him, learn to trust him and be open to his guidance at all times. For now I am calling you to push back the walls of your hearts, reach out, take my blueprint and make it a reality. Now is the time to take a leap of faith. Take a Moses leap, doing the seemingly impossible and parting the Red Sea. Take a David leap, defeating your Goliaths with one stone. Take a Peter leap by getting out of your boat and walking on water. Keep your eyes fixed on Jesus, my beloved son, so that your paths are straight and prosperous.

Quotes to Keep You Focused

Within the King's Business community at my local church we compiled the following biblical quotes to help us keep focused on God and our call to influence, and our hope is that they will also bless you:

1 John 4:4: *'You, dear children, are from God and have overcome them, because the one who is in you is greater than the one who is in the world.'*

2 Kings 6:16: *'Don't be afraid . . . Those who are with us are more than those who are with them.'*

Philippians 4:13: *'I can do all this through him who gives me strength.'*

Romans 8:28: *'And we know that in all things God works for the good of those who love him, who have been called according to his purpose.'*

Psalm 23:5: *'You prepare a table before me in the presence of my enemies. You anoint my head with oil; my cup overflows.'*

Romans 8:38–39: *'For I am convinced that neither death nor life, neither angels nor demons, neither the present nor the future, nor any powers, neither height nor depth, nor anything else in all creation, will be able to separate us from the love of God in Christ Jesus our Lord.'*

Romans 8:14–15: *'For those who are led by the Spirit of God are the children of God. The Spirit you received does not make you slaves, so that you live in fear again; rather, the Spirit you received brought about your adoption to sonship. And by him we cry, 'Abba, Father.'*

Jeremiah 1:5: *'Before I formed you in the womb I knew you, before you were born I set you apart; I appointed you as a prophet to the nations.'*

Matthew 11:30: *'For my yoke is easy and my burden is light.'*

Romans 15:13: *'May the God of hope fill you with all joy and peace as you trust in him, so that you may overflow with hope by the power of the Holy Spirit.'*

Philippians 4:7: *'And the peace of God, which transcends all understanding, will guard your hearts and your minds in Christ Jesus.'*

Further Reading

Andy Mason, *God With You at Work*, (2014), ISBN: 978-1-49226-437-8. 'God is not limited to a pulpit, but where is the tangible evidence of a supernatural God with you every day in your work?'

Mark Greene, *Thank God it's Monday*, (3rd revised edition, Scripture Union, 2001), ISBN: 978-1-85999-503-7. A practical book that looks at making the most of the time we spend with God at work.

Jim Collins, *Good to Great: Why Some Companies Make the Leap . . . And others Don't*, (Random House Business 2001), ISBN: 978-0-71267-609-0. According to Collins, humility is a key ingredient of Level 5 leadership. His simple formula is: Humility + Will = Level 5.

Daniel Goleman, *Emotional Intelligence: Why it Can Matter More Than IQ*, (Bloomsbury, 1996), ISBN: 978-0-74752-830-2. Redefines intelligence and success: excellence is more than IQ.

Jack Frost, *Spiritual Slavery to Spiritual Sonship*, (Destiny Image, 2006), ISBN: 197-0-76842-385-3. Describes how to shift from 'orphan' thinking to God's inheritance of blessings and prosperity as a child of God.

Books on the Prophetic

Jack Deere, *Surprised by the Voice of God*, (Kingsway, 2006), ISBN: 978-1-842912-85-0.

Bill Johnson, *When Heaven Invades Earth: A Practical Guide to a Life of Miracles*, (Destiny Image, 2013), ISBN: 860-1-41978-425-7.

Mark Stibbe, *Prophetic Evangelism: When God Speaks to Those Who Don't Know Him*, (Authentic, 2004), ISBN: 978-1-86024-457-5.

Phil Wilthew, *Developing Prophetic Culture*, (MDP, 2016), ISBN: 978-1-91078-647-5.

Wendy Mann, *Naturally Supernatural – The Normal Christian Life*, (MDP, 2015), ISBN: 978-1-91078-600-0.

Endnotes

1. The Chambers Dictionary, 'Management', www.chambers.co.uk (accessed 11 February 2017).

2. George Cadbury quotation, www.izquotes.com (accessed 7 February 2017).

3. https://www.cranfield.ac.uk/som/case-studies/coca-cola-enterprises-combining-profit-and-purpose

4. Pew Forum on Religion and Public, 2010.

5. *Fiddler on the Roof*, music by Jerry Bock, lyrics by Sheldon Harnick, book by Joseph Stein, set in Imperial Russia in 1905.

6. 'This Little Light of Mine' is a gospel children's song with lyrics by Avis Burgeson Christiansen and a tune written by composer and teacher Harry Dixon Loes (1895–1965) c. 1920.

7. Rodney Green, *90,000 Hours, Managing the World of Work*, (Scripture Union, 2002), ISBN: 1-85999-594-2.

8. The mountains or spheres of influence, often referred to as the 'Seven Mountains of Culture', were formulated by Francis Schaefer, Loren Cunningham and Bill Bright in 1975. See also Johnny Enlow, *The Seven Mountain Prophecy*, (Creation House, 2009), ISBN: 978-1-59979-287-3 and Lance Wallnau, *Invading Babylon: The Seven Mountain Mandate*, (Destiny Image, 2013), ISBN: 978-0-76840-335-0.

9. Heidi Baker, *Birthing the Miraculous: The Power of Personal Encounters with God to Change Your Life and the World*, (Charisma House, 2014), ISBN: 978-1-62136-219-7.

10. Marianne Williamson, 'Our Deepest Fear' from *A Return to Love: Reflections on the Principles of A Course in Miracles*, (HarperCollins, 1992), ISBN: 978-0-06016-374-7.

11. Chambers Dictionary, 'Honour', www.chambers.co.uk (accessed 11 February 2017).

12. *The Lion King* is a musical based on the 1994 Disney animated film of the same name with music by Elton John and lyrics by Tim Rice along with the musical score created by Hans Zimmer with choral arrangements by Lebo M. The original book was written by Roger Aller and Irene Mecchi.

13. Christian business network http://acalltobusiness.co.uk

14. James M. Kouzes and Barry Z. Posner, *The Leadership Challenge: How to Make Extraordinary Things Happen in Organizations*, 5th edn, (Wiley, 2012), ISBN: 978-0-47065-172-8.

15. Hans Rosling, 'The Joy of Stats', www.youtube.com/watch?v=hVimVzgtD6w (accessed 7 February 2017).

16. Mike Breen and Walt Kallestad, 'In, Up, Out Discipleship' from *A Passionate Life* (Kingsway, 2005), ISBN: 978-0-78144-269-5.

17. Chambers Dictionary, 'Honour', www.chambers.co.uk (accessed 11 February 2017).

18. Joyce Meyer, *The Everyday Life Bible: The Power of God's Word for Everyday Living*, (Hodder & Stoughton, 2006), ISBN 978-0-44657-827-1.

19. Chambers Dictionary, 'Courage', www.chambers.co.uk (accessed 11 February 2017).

20. Edward Mote, 'My Hope is Built', c. 1834.

21. Chambers Dictionary, 'Realistic', www.chambers.co.uk (accessed 11 February 2017).

22. George Müller, *The Autobiography of George Müller* (GLH Publishing, 2012).

23. *Friday the 13th* is a 1980 American slasher film directed by Sean S. Cunningham and written by Victor Miller. The film tells the story of a group of teenagers who are murdered one by one by an unknown killer while attempting to re-open an abandoned campground.